In That Sweet Country

T0040186

Books by HARRY MIDDLETON

The Earth is Enough
On the Spine of Time
The Starlight Creek Angling Society
Rivers of Memory
The Bright Country

In That Sweet Country

Uncollected Writings of
Harry Middleton

Selected and Introduced by
Ron Ellis

Skyhorse Publishing

"What mattered was the country."
—THE BRIGHT COUNTRY

"There are so few left, so few who believe
the earth is enough."
—THE EARTH IS ENOUGH

For Marcy, Travis, and Sean, and for Nick Lyons
and all the good country.

Contents

Harry Middleton:
A Brief Chronology

1949   Harry Frederick Middleton Jr., born on December 28 in Frankfurt, Germany.

1969   Graduates from Annadale High School in Annadale, Virginia.

1972   Receives Bachelor of Arts degree in history from Northwestern State University, Natchitoches, Louisiana.

1973   Receives Master of Arts degree in history (American West) from Louisiana State University, Baton Rouge.

1976   Reviews books for *Figaro*, a small, local newspaper based in New Orleans.

1980   Begins writing a weekly human-interest column for *The Advocate*, Baton Rouge.

1981   Works as a writer for *Louisiana Life*, New Orleans.

1984   Writes the "Outdoors South" column for *Southern Living* in Birmingham, Alabama, which appeared from September 1984 to January 1991.

1989   Publishes *The Earth is Enough: Growing Up in a World of Trout and Old Men*, which receives first place in the Southeastern Outdoor Press Association's "Excellence in Craft Competition-Book Category."

1990 *The Earth is Enough* wins first place in the Outdoor Writers Association of America Book Contest and receives the Friends of American Writers Award (Adult Literature).

1991 Publishes *On the Spine of Time: An Angler's Love of the Smokies.*

1992 Publishes *The Starlight Creek Angling Society.*

1993 Publishes *Rivers of Memory* and *The Bright Country: A Fisherman's Return to Trout, Wild Water, and Himself.* Dies of a massive coronary on July 28 in Hoover, Alabama, where he was cremated and buried in Jefferson Memorial Gardens near his home on Shades Mountain.

Acknowledgments

First, I am grateful to Harry Middleton's widow, Marcy Middleton Welch, for her belief in me and her support for this project, from the very first time we discussed the development of such a book. And I am grateful, too, for the advice and assistance offered by so many friends and colleagues as I gathered materials and imagined such a collection, including Jim Pruett, for too many reasons to recount; Bob Bender, Harry's editor at Simon & Schuster, for his early advice and encouragement; Mary Ellen Elsbernd and Ann Harding for their friendship and research assistance over these many years; the editors and publishers of some of our finest periodicals who first published the stories collected here, with a special thanks to Kenner Patton, managing editor of *Southern Living*, who made it possible for so many of Harry's stories from his "Outdoors South" column to appear in this collection; Lisa

Queen, Eleanor Jackson, and Emily Sklar at Queen Literary Agency for their counsel and encouragement; Tony Lyons, Kathleen Go, Kaylan Connally, and Skyhorse Publishing for making this book possible; Chuck Wechsler, publisher and editor of *Sporting Classics*, for believing in this book from the very beginning; Ashley Schroeder, the Outdoor Writers Association of America, and Lisa Snuggs, the Southeastern Outdoor Press Association, for their research assistance; the San Antonio Museum of Art for providing the Winslow Homer cover painting; Sylvia Martin for the Harry Middleton photograph; of course, Nick Lyons, who has been such a gracious mentor and friend to me and to so many other writers, and who Harry acknowledged in the dedication for *The Earth is Enough* as someone who loved "the good Earth and the good word;" and as always, my wife Debbie.

Foreword

We're at that place in time where more than ever we realize that so many things that have gone away are not coming back. Though it is also true we are always at that place. And certainly, Harry Middleton's prose is constructed of such elements. What strikes me most about reading these pieces—gathered by the diligence and commitment of author Ron Ellis—is the presence of water: flowing water, trout water, clean water. Though it is not this way, the effect it gives in memory is that such water is flowing in nearly every paragraph—that water carries many of the essays to their end—and that along the way the reader passes the secondary or ancillary element of time, geology exposed in the form of cliffs or boulders. I'm struck also by his rapturous attention to color: molten orange and bold red skies, and the dark emerald and blue-green of water. And, always, the fish: a trout's "opalescent skin flecked with shades of kingfisher blue and olive green and a pleat of color running down its flank as pink as watermelon meat."

It's interesting, seeing these pieces collected, to note the overlapping of images, similar but never repeated exactly; it is as if, for Harry Middleton, each day was new. Familiar, but then—in each breath—made somehow, slightly, new; made new with each cast, with each step.

What I admire most here then is not the pretty imagery, nor the profiles of old timers, bridges to a time long gone now and further every day, but instead something more primal: joy, and peace. The most elusive quarry of all, for many.

There is a further sweetness that attends the reading of these pieces, many of which are as small and quick as the single turn of a trout's tail, propelling it quickly into deeper water, which is this: several of these short essays were written just before Harry's death. Not to be morbid, but I find myself considering, wondering, if the body, or any part of the mind, whether conscious or not, ever intuited in any way that coming next-phase of the soul's journey. One wants to peer beneath the sentences, as if lifting cold river stones from river's bottom, and believe that one sees or senses such, in some vague way.

Still, there is only joy in these passages.

★★★

How has nearly a quarter of a century passed since his death? How is it possible that a third of a century has passed since the noodlings of some of these essays—a young man pondering fireflies, crows, whippoorwills?

Beware, O wanderer, wrote the late Jim Harrison, *the road is walking too.* What a sweet gig Harry's life appears to have been—circling round and round in the mountains, creeks, and rivers of the South, passing from season to season in a way that reminds me of another great countryman, the late John Graves.

How strange to realize that were Harry still alive, he would have become one of the old men he studied so closely and whose ways he admired; men he spent a lifetime observing, and following, just as others now follow his youthful and middle-aged prose. It's interesting, here, to read of his searches for deer, woodcock, turkey, and grouse—to read passages where, occasionally, he looks up at the stars—but as any reader knows, the truest heart of any story lies, lurks, always beneath the most inspired and graceful prose; and again and again, here, the heart of Harry's stories is cold clear mountain water, and the fish that live in it.

As I myself turn toward the country of agedness—which lies still some distance ahead, and yet, for the first time, is no longer unimaginable—I sometimes wonder briefly at the world-to-come—not mine, for I have savored so much already, and do not anticipate each next season beyond whatever splendid moment of time I inhabit—but for the future. In the lengthening span since Harry's death, we have each become more conscious of the ecological turmoil—the war against our beloved world—in which we find ourselves. The din of that battle is no longer distant. One wants to look away from a future of warmer creeks and rivers, or even no creeks or rivers. Some days we wonder what it would be like—to paraphrase Aldo Leopold—to *not* possess an ecological awareness and intelligence, so that we might be briefly innocent again.

One wonders, often, how in the world one will be able to share one's own sweet country with those who are coming afterward. I'd like to thank Ron Ellis again for the initial work in finding these essays, and Skyhorse Publishing for republishing them, and Harry's widow, Marcy, for supporting the collection, and for the lovely title. Ron isn't quite sure whether it was Harry's title or not. I almost like to think that it wasn't, but that it arose from Ron, perhaps his closest reader; and that, trained as he was in Harry's stories, the perfect title arose from the shared body of all of his work--from the common unconsciousness of it. That's the way the best writing works. That's the way words work, and the rivers that run through the woods and mountains, and the trout that rise from the depths of those rivers, seeking only to keep going.

"Still it would go deeper," he writes of one trout, his first fish, "and it went on until it nearly reached the lip of the falls before its tremendous energy was spent. I pulled it close, saw it, there in the gray water, a blur of reds and yellows, oranges and browns, and cold, black staring eyes."

That trout has gone nowhere. That trout is held in our hands forever, looking at us. It's as if time stops, in that sweet country.

—Rick Bass, April 2016

In That Sweet Country

Introduction

The idea for this book of uncollected writings by Harry Middleton originated with his readers, who, after Harry's sudden death in 1993, hungered for more of his lovable characters who were so addicted to wild trout, cold water, and mountains, "the Earth's bones," Harry called them. Because I had written the foreword for the Pruett Publishing edition of *On the Spine of Time*, often, when I was at a bookstore signing and reading from my work, one of Harry's fans would come forward and ask if I knew of any unpublished Middleton stories, hoping, I believe, for a cache of tales spun just before he died and never published. They were not ready to stop reading his stories, nor did they want him to be forgotten, now or in the future. They were hopeful, or so I thought, that I knew where to find more of the Middleton treasure they had come to rely on, to haul them into the deep quiet of the natural world and to help soothe the pain they felt at losing Harry.

I understood their need, since Harry's work meant and continues to mean a great deal to me and I, too, was deeply saddened when I learned of his death. I had been reading him for years, mostly in the early hours, before heading off to work at the university. Also, I carried around the dream that I, too, might someday be lucky enough to "live the writing life." I identified from the beginning with his often stated desire to be hauled out of this world and into the trout's, into one of those icy, gin-clear mountain streams that tugged at his heart when he was away from the mountains for too long. And I *did* know where to find some of the treasure his fans desired: it was in my basement, filed in my personal archives of Harry's many stories I had collected over the years.

When I first spoke with Harry's widow, Marcy, about assembling a selection of his previously uncollected writings, she was more than agreeable to the concept. We talked a bit about my ideas for such a book and about the kinds of stories I wanted to include—mostly his sporting tales and a few of his nature profiles, all from a variety of periodicals, including *Southern Living,* the *New York Times, Sports Illustrated, Field & Stream, Gray's Sporting Journal, Sierra,* and *Fly Rod & Reel.* Our phone conversation eventually turned toward Harry's untimely death, which led me to ask if he had been working on a new book at the time. Marcy thought she remembered that he had just started to make notes on a new book. The title of that early work-in-progress may have been, or so she thought, something similar to "In That

Sweet Country," but she couldn't be certain. She would try, she said, to find any notes Harry may have made to confirm it. Unfortunately, she could not find any written confirmation, not even a scribble, that suggested Harry was considering such a title, nor could she be absolutely certain he hadn't just casually mentioned the title as he began to imagine the story. But the title was so perfect, so much like a title he might choose for one of his books, that it didn't matter whether Marcy could authenticate it—I knew in my heart that it was pure Harry Middleton, and so I immediately adopted it for this collection.

The writings assembled here are full of the magic we have come to expect from his stories, each clearly spawned by Harry's love of memorable landscapes and the beloved characters that are always braided into and populate his writings, especially his early masterpiece, *The Earth is Enough*, followed by the very fine *On the Spine of Time*, *The Bright Country*, *Rivers of Memory*, and *The Starlight Creek Angling Society*. In these stories you will find Harry's passion for "howling whitewater" and wild trout, root beer and bacon biscuits, old men chasing something more than fish in canoes down favorite rivers, bamboo rods and bird dogs, and a selection of nature profiles as only Harry could write them, such as "Coot Du Jour," "The Bird with Brains," and "Southern Lights."

The reader will find the "germs" of stories for books to come, many featuring a familiar cast of Middleton-style characters—always genuine, always entertaining, and possibly, as Harry tells us in *On the Spine of Time*, "more real than imagined." And there is a rare poem, "Buffalo River Sequence," from *Sierra*, the only poem by Middleton

I have ever seen published, although Marcy said he wrote a good deal of poetry over the years. There is also a fine story about collectible bamboo rods, titled "Classic Cane," which first appeared in *Fly Rod & Reel* under the *nom de plume* Churchill Payne, and, according to Marcy, is only one of Harry's many pen names. To that list, she said, we could add Dean McClain, Paul Sneider, and Emerson Trout. Harry also worked as a ghost writer and co-author on a variety of publishing projects, including co-writing, with fly-fishing legend Lefty Kreh, the Lyons Press's popular *Lefty's Favorite Fly-Fishing Waters.*

Books played a prominent role in Harry's life and tales, as much as the rivers, wild trout, mountains, and "slants of light" he required. In *The Earth is Enough*, young Harry, shortly after arriving in Arkansas, discovers Emerson and Albert's large and diverse collection of books housed in their farmhouse at "Trail's End." We see at first a treasure trove of old photographs hanging about the rooms, miscellaneous outdoor gear, and an array of personal memorabilia. Later, we are treated to Harry's first glimpse of the "big room" and his discovery of its treasure—a vast library of hundreds of books stacked, shelved, and scattered across the entire space—equaling, he tells us, "the holdings of a modest library."

"Everywhere I looked," he says, "books struggled for space, dominance, attention, the life readers alone can give them."

"Where to start?" he asks.

Indeed, where to start.

Whether you are a longtime Middleton fan, or just discovering his stories, I think you will find this collection most gratifying. And if you are lucky enough to be a brand new Middleton fan, then I'm envious, as you have all of his wonderful books yet to read.

So, here's the treasure I found for you, a fine selection of Harry's stories that will haul you into that sweet country he so often led us to throughout his life.

—Ron Ellis
Townsend, Tennessee
November 2009

ARKANSAS

The Fisherman

It was an April morning, although it could have been any one of a score of spring mornings among the low, gray-backed Boston Mountains of Arkansas. It was one of those days when the land, finally letting loose of winter, began to take hold of the sun's new warmth. My grandfather had a small, white frame house in these mountains. The house was set back off the old blacktop road, all but hidden by thick boysenberry bushes that the old man steadfastly refused to interfere with. Every room of the little house smelled of the old man and the mountains, of compost and wild ginger, plug chewing tobacco and ripe blueberries, purple-hull beans and the fresh, damp odor of pine after a summer downpour.

On April mornings, long before dawn, the house was filled with the hissing of the kettle. My grandfather, in overalls and slippers, was down in the kitchen enveloped by a cloud of steam, standing over a metal teakettle with a pair of long needle-nose pliers, rejuvenating trout flies, a ritual that announced spring as surely as the robin's return, the peeper's call, the first crocus bloom. As the days lengthened and the earth warmed, the small creeks and streams that run through the Boston Mountains began to ripple with new life. In their cool, fast waters millions of insects waited for just the right slant of the sun, just the right temperature to hatch. Also waiting, their sleek noses pointed upstream, were the trout, their round eyes surveying the stream's surface for any movement, the smallest flutter of an insect's wing.

The old man began preparing for these April mornings months before when the wind was still strong out of the north and the land and the streams were frozen. Fishing, he believed, like gardening, demanded constant care and attention. He never stopped thinking of fish and fishing, even during winter's bleakest days. Not long after Christmas he began his daily visits to the small shed at the corner of the house.

There he kept his rods and reels, his silk lines, gut leaders, creel, and the small cherrywood cabinet in which he stored his flies and fishing tools: pliers, razor blades, assorted tweezers, pocketknives, a pair of stainless-steel forceps given to him by a doctor in town. Like most trout fishermen he collected just about everything, from piano wire to old thread spools, on the theory that catching fish, and especially trout, demands large doses of imagination and ingenuity. He spent countless hours in the shed varnishing his rods, oiling his reels, seeing to it that his gut leaders were moist and properly stowed, cleaning and sharpening his hooks, patching his waders. And he spent hours arranging his flies according to the species, habitat, and likely time of appearance of the insect imitated. In a small, black leather case lined with yellow flannel, he kept his favorite flies, the ones he had caught fish with and those he dreamed of catching fish with. Like a taxidermist, the old man examined and groomed these flies, arranged them one way, then another, and discarded the worn and luckless ones. But the names and number remained the same. March Brown and Red Quill, Quill Gordon and Dun Variant, Sulfur Dun and Pale Evening Dun, stone fly and Woolly Worm, Green Drake and Royal Coachman, caddis and caddis pupa, Rat-Faced McDougal.

When he could not fish, or on winter evenings after his work was done, he would settle down at the kitchen table with the latest fishing magazines and catalogues. My grandfather dearly loved shopping the catalogues for odd pieces of equipment and innovative, promising-looking flies. He spent many an evening filling his tackle box by mail. Once the catalogues and magazines were searched through, exhausted, he eagerly turned to his favorite books, to authors like Roderick Haig-Brown and Ernest Hemingway. The old man loved to tell me that there was more to fishing than hooking a fish. Anyone could do that. Fishing went deeper. Fishing, the old man earnestly believed, was a way for man to reconnect with the natural world. A man with a fishing pole in his hands became just one creature among many, each trying to outwit the other. Fishing put a man back into nature's economy, made him a participant, not just an observer. Hemingway and the others were full of such intimations, fine stuff for the old fisherman's winter dreams.

⇢◦⇠

Soon enough the April sun came, and the old man shook me awake before dawn. We ate biscuits and drank coffee at the kitchen table and said nothing. He liked listening to the dawn and was eager to feel the day's weather and try to gauge it, to judge it as the trout might. On such mornings his weak blue eyes seemed brighter behind his thick wire-rimmed glasses.

He had chosen our destination, Blue Rock Creek, months before. It was a stream whose name and location, well north through the mountains, he had picked up through gossip or from his magazine reading. All streams were special to the old man. They were worlds tucked within worlds, a mysterious and wondrous rush of water and life. He loved the smell and feel of mountain streams and had an idea that if life could be touched, it would feel something like a fast-running mountain stream.

For the old man, getting to know a stream—reading its water and locating its fish—was perhaps the most enjoyable part of fishing. Walking a stream and observing it were matters of the utmost importance and practicality, like picking up a rod, resting it in the palm of your hand, and testing its bend and weight before buying it.

With the old Ford truck parked well off the road and unloaded, he walked into the water of Blue Rock Creek and sank down into its cold water. He once told me that he liked trout fishing above all other fishing because trout fishermen aren't afraid to get in the water with the fish. How else could you find the cold spots, the hidden deep pools rich in oxygen and big fish? After assessing the Blue Rock from that angle, he walked its grassy banks noting the sunken logs and branches, the good cover where there was an abundance of frogs and insects and, possibly, fish.

The sun was up now and a breeze came off the stream. He took his rod and creel, entered the creek, and began walking upstream, presenting his fly to the fish as nature presents the insect. He fished without haste or frustration, but steadily, patiently. He worked each quarter of the Blue Rock, each pool, each spot where a fish might wait.

As so often happened on those spring mornings, I soon stopped fishing and sat on the stream bank in the shade of the trees to watch him. He was both the man and the fisherman I wanted to become, and watching him, thigh-deep in the Blue Rock, effortlessly casting his line, seemed just the pastime for a boy in the spring. Aside from the hard-boiled egg I peeled and took out to him, he passed up lunch and kept casting. As the day got hot, he would dip his old cap into the creek, set it back on his head, and let the cold water run down his face, down the deep lines he had worked into his skin.

Late in the afternoon the wind shifted back 'round to the north and the rain came, slow, steady, soaking. It was the kind of rain that stirs insects and fish and fishermen. The old man's pace quickened. Rain dripping from the bill of his cap, he put even more energy and determination into his casts. Suddenly a swarm of insects rose like a cloud from the stream's surface. With no hint of excitement the old man moved his hand through this cloud of insects and caught one, noted its size and color, took his black leather case from inside his fishing vest, selected the fly that most resembled the captured mayfly, tied it to his leader, and cast.

Nothing.

Again, nothing.

Another cast and then it hit, a large trout taking the fly even before it settled on the water's surface. The fish was a mosaic of reds and browns, golds, whites, and blues—the colors of every stone it had rubbed against. The fish rose and twisted, ran, jerked wildly, doubled back, exhausted, and finally, lay at the old man's feet. My grandfather bent down and lifted his big trout with his landing net, held it up and looked at it, touched its thick flanks, then carefully removed the hook, letting the fish go. Then he wiped the rain from his glasses, wrung out his cap, tied on another fly, and cast.

The rain ended as suddenly as it began, moving down the valley and leaving the old man shrouded in mist. The air cooled, deep purple shadows gathered among the young willows and pin oaks, and the old man tossed his line once more against the setting sun.

(1983)

First Fish

No matter how many years pass, no matter the impressive collage of angling experiences a fisherman gathers within him, some memories give way to others. It happens to all anglers. Eventually, the fish caught easily on a bright and clear day, a handsome but modest fish, becomes, after a decade of soaking in the imagination's brine, a piscatorial leviathan taken on a dark and stormy day, the creek lashing about like a storm-tossed sea. In the end, after the noble fish had straightened out the hook and broken line, rod, and reel, you had to wrestle him singlehandedly to the creek bank, and it took all your strength to lift the great fish because it surely weighed 30 pounds or better.

This is one of the great charms of angling. It, like fine wine, improves with age. But there is an exception, a memory, a fish, that for every angler is never again equaled or "bested." And that is the memory of the first fish.

That first fish ever rises in the mind and imagination, and there again you feel the adrenaline pour into your blood. It is a sensation, once felt, that stays with an angler forever, keeping him company even on the days when there are no fish, when work and obligation keep him from angling.

My first fish was a trout. A brown trout. Taken on my great-uncle Albert's Orvis cane fly rod up along the upper reaches of Starlight Creek in the Ozark Mountains of Arkansas.

Cold October morning. Gray light. Good signs, at least for brown trout. I asked Albert if I could borrow his fly rod, the one I would buy some months later for $5. The old man smiled.

"Okay," he said, "but you gotta talk to it. It's the best fishing partner a man could want 'cause no matter what you say, it agrees. It never talks back. Least ways it hasn't in these 20 or 30 years."

I gathered up the rod and reel and my jacket. My grandfather wrapped up a hot biscuit and sausage patty, stuffed the little bundle in my pocket.

Down past the old barn, past the far end of the great garden lush then with collards and turnips, the trail turned, followed the creek. I headed upstream, up toward Karen's Pool. The creek, full of winter rain, moaned and hissed, groaned as it rushed over the smooth backs of dark stones. The clouds overhead gave the creek an opaque finish, dull and dreary. And the wind came harder and colder.

I spoke to the old rod, commenting on the weather. It was good trout weather indeed. Surely, the browns would be on the move, for they are a moody and deeply suspicious member of the trout family, uncomfortable in direct sunlight, in any light that betrays their presence. They are fish of deeper, colder water; fish of cloud-choked days; trout of rain and storm, dull mornings, and dreary twilights. I tied on a medium-size streamer fly, worked out maybe 25 feet of line, cast gently, laid line, leader, and tippet out as cleanly as my awkward talent allowed, hoping the current would carry the fly as naturally as it carried a drowned leaf or a shard of broken twig, carry it toward the browns.

I cast the streamer fly again, working out more line, casting up and across the stream, using the current and a tight eddy swirling around a bent archipelago of stones on the far side of the creek. I had seen the largest shadow there. A wrinkle just below the surface of the water that looked as long as my arm.

Another cast, the icy water numbing my feet and calves, tugging relentlessly at me, urging me downstream. Morning settled in the narrow valley, became a study in the range and limits of the color gray.

Then, suddenly, that weight on the line, the tip of the old Orvis rod bending in a dangerous bow. Strangely, the moment did not freeze or even cycle down in my mind's eye to slow motion. Rather, the flow of the experience continued sweeping me along with it. I hauled the trout toward my world: it hauled me into its world. And I got the better of destinations.

Each time I would take in line, pull the trout toward the surface, thinking surely I had it now. Still, it would go deeper, and it went on until it nearly reached the lip of the falls before its tremendous energy was spent. I pulled it close, saw it there in the gray water, a blur of reds and yellows, oranges and browns, and cold, black staring eyes.

I reached down, working the fly from its jaw carefully. My hands were shaking. Trout give you the shakes, men and boys alike, whether it's their first trout or their hundredth.

I stood in the cold creek for some time. I tried to cast, but couldn't. My energy, too, was spent, and I walked on out of the creek and back to the house slowly, rethinking, reliving it all over and over.

I still dream of that morning and that trout, and every dream, after all these years, adds some new detail. This past fall I dreamed of it all again and remembered something that I had not remembered since that cold, gray Arkansas morning so long ago—that when the brown trout took the fly, I shouted loud and hard.

(1990)

Downriver, Again

The morning is cold under a thick, hard-bottomed sky. A freezing drizzle promises sleet, maybe snow. We labor through clouds of our own breath. The old man and I carry the eighteen-foot Grumman canoe to the river's edge. The old man, dressed in worn overalls, a sweat-stained blue bandanna, lampblack high-top tennis shoes, and a creased mole-brown fedora, is my grandfather, an Arkansas farmer. The early hours of the morning were spent butchering a sow named Widow Fay, and there are still clots of frozen pig blood on the old man's shirt sleeves. The river is up, gunmetal blue and restless. We carried the dented canoe six miles downstream from the town of Boxley, Arkansas. The old man will not drive his 1952 Ford pickup truck into the woods this close to the headwaters of the river. The noisy truck scares off the animals, tramples young willows and catalpas, leaves scars, tracks. The old man wants no one to know where he is or how to find him. He is on the river. That is enough. He stops hauling gear to gather some vacant spider webbing from the branches of a dead elm. He rolls the sticky silk into a ball with his palms and eats it. Good, he says, for his asthma.

The Grumman is, as always, packed lightly. This is a journey, not an expedition. We have come for what the river still offers freely, abundantly: peace, wildness, reassurance. We keep our load simple: a change of clothes, tarpaulin, matches, skillet, tobacco, beans, peanut butter, a tin of raw honey, sourdough, bacon, hardtack, Cutter's snakebite kit, coffee, and a jar of Vicks VapoRub—the one ointment most insects detest more than they like the sweet taste of human blood. A wind builds among the hardwoods, sets in the bones like a double-bent fishhook. Near the opposite bank a rock bass breaks the surface, a shiny blur against the morning's blue mist. All along the river everything is stretching, yawning, stirring, impatient with new life. Near a weathered brown stone a patch of Dutchman's breeches has the audacity to bloom; overhead a broad-winged, red-winged hawk circles, waiting for something below to wiggle. He screams *keer-keer-keer*. His breakfast call. Here, concealed by thick woods on both banks, hemmed in by narrow ravines and rock-strewn gorges, the Buffalo River looks like a dark and bulging capillary wrinkling against translucent flesh. The old man pushes us off from the shore and into the river's mercurial current, sets his ash-wood paddle in the canoe, lights his pipe, settles in.

I like the river best at this time of year, before the May crowds, when it is distended by winter rains, boisterous, full of itself, flexing its muscle, racing down the northern face of the ancient Boston Mountains. In three months its boyish energy will be exhausted; the wild, tail-less kite will fall; the river will be older, slower, lazier, drier, hardly more than a stream in a river's bed, as awkward as a boy trying on his father's pants. But now the river is all surprise and potential; it can fool you at any time, turn mean and let indifference loose—a slashing tongue of silt and rock and dismembered trees. A sudden afternoon thunderstorm can easily leave you clinging to the crown of an oak, water at your socks and rising, while turning your canoe into a tin acrobat performing arching somersaults all the way to Buffalo City.

The old man knows what the river can do, keeps an eye on markings he has made over the years along the river. He remembers the day in 1915 when, caught in a boiling storm, the Buffalo rose fifty feet in less than twenty-four hours, surged out of its small valley, and went looking for trouble. The Buffalo is not like the Colorado, the Salmon, the Rio Grande, the Allagash. It is a small and intimate river, at its widest point hardly more than a hundred yards across, and for years its lack of reputation among thrill seekers kept it safe, unnoticed. Although the Buffalo River valley has an Indian history that goes back more than nine-thousand years, the land surrounding the river was not settled by anyone but itinerant farmers and trappers and miners until the early twentieth century. Before World War II, zinc and lead deposits were discovered in the valley, but the veins proved thin and were soon mined out. The loggers came and went, as disappointed as the miners: the valley simply could not turn a profit. Only the determined farmers stayed. Left to itself, the river healed, continued to run free and clean. Now, all that is changing—and quickly. Saved from a proposed damming of its upper reaches above Gilbert, mainly through the work of the Ozark Society, and made a national river in 1972 by presidential order, the Buffalo has become a celebrity, a recreational river.

Since 1972 the National Park Service has managed to purchase 90 percent of the 95,370 acres of the land designated to be set aside in the 1972 proclamation, but not without considerable trouble. Many of those who have lived all their lives along the river have given up their land grudgingly, vengefully; others continue to hang on. Meanwhile, the crowds keep coming, getting larger and larger each year. Last year, as far as the rangers can tell, the river was visited by more than 576,000 people. Some rangers believe that as many as a million tourists will visit the Buffalo this year. And of course the river has attracted the usual clutter of tourism's camp followers—land developers ("Own a Piece of the Scenic Buffalo"), fast-food restaurants, campgrounds, gift shops, guides, outfitters (twenty-four licensed float operators now operate along the river), and roads and more roads to accommodate the cars and more cars. The fifteen full-time rangers, whose thankless job it is to patrol 132 twisting miles of river, spend most of their time not tracking down vandals but taking reservations, counting heads, keeping records, giving directions to the restrooms. Saved, the Buffalo is no longer a wilderness but a theme park, an industry expected to turn a profit and earn its keep. The Buffalo is free to go its own way only so long as it obeys the rules and properly entertains the thousands upon thousands who clog the mountain roads every summer to see it, barbecue beside it, play in it, float potato-chip bags down it, and mill about the campgrounds wondering why this wilderness doesn't have better showers, more vending machines, a game room, nightly bingo.

Above Ponca the old man and I come upon a sign in the shape of an arrow pointing downstream. It is nailed to the trunk of a chinquapin. The sign reads in large red letters: "Buffalo Point Park 42 Mi." The old man steers the canoe up under the tree, works the sign loose, tosses it back into the brush. "There were no signs here in 1907 when I first did the river," he tells me calmly, "and there will be no signs here the last time I am on it." The old man is a romantic, incurable and incalculable.

At this time of the year, in this weather, we are not likely to see anyone else on the river. But we have the company we want—a few deer, beaver, green sunfish and needle-nose gar, muskrat, green herons, and always, the nasty-tempered rattling of kingfishers skimming the river's surface for an easy meal. This is what we were counting on. We are selfish travelers and want the river, all of it, for ourselves. We want the sound of river water buffeting smooth rock, the thrill of a cloudless afternoon sky, the river valley's enduring present. The river moves on and on and we follow, willingly.

———⋙◆⋘———

The Buffalo River begins near Fallsville, Arkansas, runs fast and hard down the flanks of the Boston Mountains, and is eventually joined by the Little Buffalo River near Ponca. Here the river cuts into the sandstone of the Springfield

Plateau near Erbie Ford below the town of Pruitt and then twists and turns for more than 130 miles through Newton, Searcy, and Marion counties before it joins the forever eerie and cold and shrouded water of the White River near Buffalo City. The Buffalo bends and feeds an old valley of caves, waterfalls, abandoned mines and homesteads, giant granite bluffs that rise 500 feet above the river in some places, deep tangles of oak and hickory, cedar and shortleaf pine, silver maple and willow, sycamore, catalpa, and the shrubby little chinquapin.

By evening of the first day out we are near Big Bluff, the river's grandest peak, its big show. The weather has broken, revealing a salmon-pink sky edging back toward the horizon. The day seems to evaporate and night comes down the valley like a curious army of shadows stalking every splash of light. We pull the canoe onto shore, hike up to the Goat Trail, which is about 360 feet up the face of Big Bluff, rest, have a cup of coffee. "From here a man can see just all he needs to see," the old man says. It is what he always says from this spot. I nod, not wanting to spoil the deep quiet. On the river I am all sense and exposed nerve, content with life's surface and chaos, its every poke and prod, the exultation of its every whisper and detail. We make camp near a gutted cabin at Hemmen-in-Hollow. The river hangs on to the day's last shafts of light, gathering them into small pools of brilliant color and form, which look like distant galaxies blinking sadly in a late summer sky. Tiny saw-whet owls are out serenading field mice in the tall grass by the river, waiting for one of them to doze off. Already knowing the inevitable outcome of their song, the owls are patient, but the grass trembles with nervous mice.

The night is full of predators sniffing the air for dinner's scent. Large, evil-looking mosquitoes join us by the fire, begin creeping down our socks to get at our ankles. Time for the Vicks. Across the river a raccoon descends from a dead oak, looks both ways before setting foot to earth, then disappears, becoming sound and shadow. The moon hangs deep in the Arkansas night—a night filled with the old man's songs and old jokes, the sweet smell of burning birch, the mosquitoes' whir, and finally, the old man's even snoring. Sleep is easy and deep, and I am awakened by the smell of coffee, beans, bacon, sourdough cakes. I bathe in the river, reveling in its cold sting. A sycamore leaf falls belly-up in the river's mirror surface, and a damselfly settles on it, certain it is paradise and all she needs, for the moment.

This morning the river's voice is a contralto of slaps and whistles, the trill of riffles over rock gardens, and the dull whacking of white water. We pack the canoe and drift. Any other way of life that has a claim on me slips away from me like dead skin. The rapids are easy, and through them the old man keeps puffing on his pipe and talking. I listen and think that this is all I need or will ever need—the river, wood, wind, the sound of the sun rising, the old man, his pipe and spider webbing, this painfully elusive now, where everything is at once old and new, true to itself, sure of itself, always beginning, ending, and beginning again. It is difficult to go down a river, any river, for the hundredth time and not become an oracle, ready to speak of its untapped promise and possibility, its wondrous mystery and actuality.

We ease our canoe past the hump-backed rock and gravel shoals near Mount Hersey, down past Cane Bluff,

Welch Bluff, Big Creek, where we have a lunch of M&Ms, honey, and raisins—the last of the bacon. We spend the rest of the day watching river striders and soaking up the river's every gesture, offhand remark, smallest detail. The second night's sleep, on a stony gravel bar, is even deeper, more restful than the first. Morning breaks clear and remorseless. Up ahead is Woolum and Gilbert, not the end of the river but of our sojourn on it, this time. We negotiate Horseshoe Rock rapids taking on water for the first time, pass White Spring, Whisnant Bluff, Calf Creek, Rocky Hollow, Tyler Bend. Below Tyler Bend is the Highway 65 bridge. Gilbert is four miles downstream. Gilbert is noted for its bad weather, good gossip, and for Baker's General Store, which has a telephone.

The old man steers us in, jumps out, and heads for Baker's and the latest news and candy bars. I empty the canoe, turn it over in the river several times—washing out the sand, gravel, spent tobacco, tadpoles, twigs, a brown spider—and pull it up on the bank and sit. The afternoon sky is on fire, and the river valley is the color of polished copper. The old man comes back with two Hershey bars and fresh rumor. Someone has told him that a man from up around Beech Creek had strapped himself into his johnboat, determined on one last ride. He was found, the story went, hands bound in front with bootlaces, washed up near Jackpot Bluff, seventeen miles below Gilbert.

"Imagine that," said the old man. "Nice way to go, all told. Word is he had cancer of some kind and was bound for death. Better to let the river have you on a stormy night. Faster, surer, no pain. Nice way to go. Perhaps the best. Fellow up at the store tells how he heard crazy laughter coming off the river some nights back. Probably that old man in the johnboat finding it funny to end up at Jackpot."

The old man got a lift back upriver to the truck. I waited on the highway, sitting on the overturned canoe. There was a new hawker on the other side of the road selling T-shirts that boasted "I Survived the Buffalo River." As the evening shadows began to edge out of the wood and across the highway, I wondered if the Buffalo will survive us, all of us.

(1981)

Buffalo River Sequence: A Poem

I

Barely more than a scattering of hog-backed hills
Cluttered with olive-colored stones,
The mountains rise out of the low Arkansas countryside
ill-defined,
The first meager outcroppings drawing *little* notice until
the straight
Road narrows, wrinkles out of the smooth land.
Curves tighten; the roadbed steepens; cobalt-green canyon
rims
Take shape in the distance.
Mountains endure, the hard, lasting substance of time and
shadow;
The Earth's bones.

II

Below the desolate clapboard remains of the Red Cloud
mine,
Where the zinc played out, and disappointed, weary
miners
Picked up, moved on, another dream in their haversack,
The river glides easily over burnished rock,
Bends insouciantly between high granite bluffs,
past knots
Of boulders exposed by low water.
Stillness takes on shape, definition:
A small wind stirs among the trees; the river moves on
And on; the heart follows, willingly, always glad to be
Hunter, discoverer.

III

A hissing comes out of the hush from below the deserted
mine.
Ahead, the river, pinched-in by jagged banks and rock,
Races through a gorge strewn with sunken logs and
porcine stones
Gleaming under the roiling, rushing water like blue-steel
traps.
Suddenly enraged, the river grasps the canoe's sleek
metallic hull,
Throws it forward. The river's anger loosens a tired face,
Dull eyes, fills the body, every joint, muscle and nerve,
with expectation.
Cracked lips are licked, wetted again and again.
The thwacking, cachunking noise of the river gets louder,
louder.

Slack water is hacked, ripped, beat and rent open
By ragged piles of rock and wood. The body has no
emotion, no thought,
Is ripe with feeling and instinct. Currents have swelled to
sea-waves:
On the river every moment is now, a wild, dizzying dance
of constant creation.

IV

Above Gosha Creek the river widens;
The clamor of racing white water eases;
The body cools, rejoices at having been briefly pure motion,
Pushed beyond existence and into the bright cell of the
river's timelessness.
There comes rapid, triumphant breathing and a complete
And wonderful exhaustion.
Beyond the high canyon rims, night begins to slice up the
afternoon
With deep shadows, and a breeze comes off the river.
The river holds onto small pools of refracted, flecked light;
It will give up the day but not its warmth.

V

I imagine explorers, trappers—
Marquette, Joliet, La Salle, Hugh Glass,
James Beckwourth, Antoine Leroux—
Knee deep in uncharted, nameless rivers.
Shading their eyes from the same morning sun, Indian
canoes strung out
Behind them, they stand at the water's edge
in the still air

Of a hundred mountain valleys, wondering
what secrets the rivers
Beyond their sight hold, nourish,
What mysteries they bleed into.
Anticipation corrupts the silence,
And they move on, each one smiling.

(1983)

Trout

There are three spruce paddles in the canoe. I always lose at least one, but I do not mind. Paddles are a small price to pay for such mornings and for the promise of not just any fish, but trout. The sky is clear, and there are only a few high clouds as thin as an old man's whiskers. The sun is barely above the Boston Mountains, and already the temperature is 80 degrees. Summer settles into this river valley quickly and with no mercy. Small winds build among the hardwoods at the river's edge and smell of wild dogwood. I slept last night under a bright white Arkansas moon below a granite cliff known on the Buffalo River as Elephant Head Rock, which is less than a day's paddle from the White River. The White River is where the trout are, rainbows and cutthroats. Rain has been scarce this year, leaving the Buffalo hardly more than a damp crack between the mountains. Logs and stumps have surfaced all along the river, looking like brown and brittle ghosts, and the river bottom resembles an unlucky miner's sluice—all gravel and rock. The canoe drags the bottom through the narrow riffles, making a sound like iron nails dragged across slate. The only sounds louder are the birds, fat wood thrushes, ornery kingfishers, and fish crows.

The White River is felt before it is seen. All of a sudden a chill soaks the air. Socks and shoes shed because of the Buffalo's heat are hurriedly put back on; the aluminum canoe begins to sweat. A shroud of mist hangs inches above the White, always, and the water's temperature rarely rises above 50 degrees, even in late summer. In such an unsteady climate light and color change not by the hour but by the minute. Each turn, each spring, each pool here is a separate world. Where I take my paddle from the river the water is china-blue; where I put it in again the water is deep zinc green. And up ahead it is as dark as black cherry bark. Above the valley, cold lightning, high in energy but of short duration, creates great razor tracks across the sky.

The trout are here. I can almost feel them hugging the bottom, their weight against the current. They have waited this long, I think; they can wait until after lunch, which today is a sandwich made of breakfast's leftover bacon, the last of the lemon-flavored Gookinaid, and an apple. I am eager for the trout, though, and leave half the apple uneaten. For me, an angler proud of his amateur standing and determined to keep it, there is no other fish but trout. My affair with trout is one of love and wonder that began with boyhood and shows no signs of abating. Then, as now, fishing was part of each day's adventure. I have never weighed a fish or put a tape measure to one or kept a record of my catches any more than I have kept a record of every bird I have seen on the wing. I am always too busy either fishing or observing to count or measure things. My grandfather taught me early on to travel light and that fish will take a worm as quickly from a hastily cut cane pole as from a $500 fly rod. Gear, the old man never tired of telling me, improves an angler's chances, not his skill. For years my tackle box was a pocket tobacco tin in which I kept a suitable length of line, usually a piece of 4-pound-test, a No.8 hook, a sinker, and a Barlow pocket knife. Unencumbered, I wandered and explored at my ease and fished whenever fortune led me to a pond or stream. I took my first trout with the gear of my tobacco tin, a cut pole, and a fresh and fat summer grasshopper. No other fish since, despite a heavy influx of gear, has fought as hard, looked as grand, or tasted as good.

Trout are an easy fish to admire. Small, tentative, secretive, moody, cautious, running from the slightest portent of trouble, even sudden shadows. They are hard to fool, too, and are stubborn about not taking flies that look like Easter hats rather than caddisfly nymphs. The rainbow trout of the White seem to be all color down to their pearl-white bones and chalk-white flesh. Two years ago on this river I took a small rainbow trout that truly glowed in the morning sunlight, its nearly opalescent skin flecked with shades of kingfisher blue and olive green and a pleat of color running down its flank as pink as watermelon meat. This fish seemed to be the source of the river's color, for when I took him, the water perceptively dulled from bright green to brown. I let him go, gladly.

Perhaps the best thing about trout is that they give anglers such long periods of silence and genuine privacy, time to consider rocks, time to float an idea as well as a fly, time to let emotions drift as freely as the current. Trout lead a man who will follow into another time and place, a place of rock and water, air and sky, shifting river bottom and quiet temperament. The picky trout of the White have given me nearly all of the precious late-afternoon hours to follow these thoughts while wading upstream through the river's pools and riffles, away from the main channel. Trout are like the river; they never stop moving. I have changed flies four times. Still, nothing, save the light snapping sound of the bamboo pole slicing the air, the sight of the gently drifting fly, the feel of the river bottom sucking at my boots. Somewhere deep in the stands of oak and hackberry an owl screeches: night's signal. On cue, long shadows dance down the valley floor. One more cast. Nothing. Well, one more. Nothing. Across from where I stand there is the sudden sound of disturbed water, of jump and splash. For an instant the shadows shimmer and I catch sight of a trout's cream-white throat held for an instant against the rising moon. Tomorrow, I have an old No. 8 hook in my creel, and the tall grass along the river is alive with the bow-saw chorus of fat, fresh summer grasshoppers.

(1983)

The Ozarks: Where the Big Trout Run

It has been a rainy winter. The rivers are wide and fast, and the citrine waters are swift and cold. Up from the deep green pools, the hump-backed, rigid Ozark Mountains roll north toward the Missouri state line like an exposed backbone. The Ozarks are truly ancient, the remnants of a primeval seafloor that dates back perhaps 450 million years. As mountains go, compared to the hoary Ozarks, the Alps and the Himalayas are but geologic children.

After a wet winter, Bull Shoals Lake is full and strong, and the dams on the White and North Fork Rivers are opened daily. The rivers change character easily, too, like faucets under different pressures. With the dams off and the rivers down, they take on a calm, even tranquil disposition.

This is especially true of the North Fork. Propelled by modest currents, it meanders insouciantly along its length. Now, it moves quietly, stretches of quiet water and deep, inviting pools, and faster narrow riffles, water hemmed in by gravel bars. The blue-green water holds sunlight like a jewel, is translucent except for the deeper pools where its color is a darker emerald green. Trout lie everywhere along the river's course. Rainbows flash upstream, iridescent flanks undulating in the current, their muscled bodies positioned upstream. Unabated hunger leaves them restless, constant hunters. Beneath the large, smooth boulders, hiding patiently among the tendrils of brush and downed trees and stumps, in the camouflage of shadow and fickle light, are the big browns. Tenacious, implacable carnivores, they linger, as if knowing that time and fate favored them. Their muddy-dark skin is spectacularly splashed with a haunting array of colored splotches, flecks of oxblood reds and waxy yellows. These rivers hold cutthroat trout as well. Like rainbows, cutthroats are Western trout that have done well in these cold Ozark rivers and now thrive here. The cutthroats, some reaching tremendous sizes of more than 5 to 10 pounds, are known not so much for their size as for their noble character and their wild blood, their unbending truculence.

The generators on the North Fork have been shut down for two days, leaving a mild-mannered river of even disposition. Trout congregate in the pools and riffles. They are easily observed by walking slowly and quietly to the edge of an exposed gravel bar, dozens of them magnified by the clear, cold water so that even the smallest among them seems a significant and worthy fish. They remain clearly visible, barely a cast away, feeding hungrily on the great bounty of insect larvae found in the nutrient-rich moss that covers the river bottom. We work the pool upstream and across, taking advantage of the calm water and the riffle that transects the pool. In less than half an hour, we catch and release more than ten rainbow trout, none of them weighing less than 3 pounds, and at least one 5-pounder, all of them strong, healthy, beautiful trout. We work our way to the next pool, casting the supple fly line as we go, working every foot of water. There is only the squawk of a lone kingfisher along the riverbank, the reflection of the warming sunlight off the river, and the hushed, muted sound of the fly line moving effortlessly through the air. Gradual and splendid, the sunset is a drama of light, a tapestry of bold reds and molten oranges in a cloudless Ozark sky. Along the bluffs by the river, lengthening purple shadows cloak the ridgelines, spill over toward the horizon.

At dawn, we move on to Gaston's White River Resort, which sits on a small rise overlooking the big river. More and more such resorts open each year along the alluring and beautiful rivers and lakes of the Ozarks. The land is that raw, that tempting, that beautiful. The fishing is that good.

Of the many Arkansas Ozark fishing resorts, Gaston's remains one of the most popular and most respected, operating in an atmosphere of hospitality and comfort where an angler can enjoy a great river and the always-intoxicating presence of trout—big trout.

Gaston's is also one of the oldest of the Ozark fishing resorts. Jim Gaston opened the lodge in 1958 along a White River that had changed a good deal. Before the construction of the Bull Shoals Dam in 1951, the White had been a warm-water bass river. The dam, however, changed the river's character. What had been a warm river became a cold river, with the average year-round temperature hovering at about 48 degrees. Bass water became trout water, water that then offered superior fishing throughout the year. Arkansas undertook an aggressive and well-managed trout-stocking program, and within a decade, the White and the North Fork Rivers had earned a reputation of offering perhaps the South's most consistent and challenging trout fishing.

Located 15 miles from Mountain Home, Gaston's White River Resort soon became a mecca for gypsy trout fishermen from throughout the South and around the country. Fishing news travels fast among anglers, like electricity through copper wire, and the news about Gaston's was simple. All who came and who fished spread the word:

It was a piscatorial paradise. Beautiful country. Friendly people. Good food. And most important, trout that hit like uncoupled freight cars.

Gaston's has seventy-one different accommodations, boasts a 3,200-foot private airstrip, and employs thirty fishing guides. Although a boat is assigned to each cottage, guests are urged to use a guide. The White is big, powerful, and extremely unpredictable.

While fishing can be excellent throughout the year, Gaston's most productive season runs from April through October. The rainy season usually determines how the river will run. If rainfall is normal, explains Ron Branaman, resort manager, the river's high-water month usually comes in the spring. Among trout fishermen, the White is noted not only for the consistent quality of its trout fishing but for the size of its trout as well. Many an angler's imagination is haunted by images of monster White River and North Fork River trout. On these rivers, trophy rainbow trout can reach weights of 20 pounds or more. Indeed, 5-pound rainbows, truly respectable trout on any trout river in the nation, are common residents in these Ozark rivers. Too, the moody browns often reach unbelievable sizes—15, 20, 25, 30 pounds and more. Because of their large populations of big trout, the White, the North Fork, and the other Ozark trout streams and rivers attract many fishermen obsessed with taking a trophy-sized fish.

Increasing fishing pressures on these big trout had convinced lodge owners and local guides in the 1970's to form the White and North Fork River Outfitter's Association, a group devoted to maintaining the beauty of the Ozark rivers and the integrity of their unsurpassed trout fishing. Of the association's many aims, none is more vital than its dedication to a catch-and-release program for all of the Ozark's trout waters. While no angler is refused a trophy fish, one he can mount on his wall, the association encourages all anglers to release their trophy-size catches, all trout over 4 pounds. All this does not mean that Ozark trout can be caught but never completely enjoyed. The White and the North Fork are regularly and amply stocked with rainbow trout so that every fisherman has the chance to take his limit of 1- and 2- and 3-pounders. While rainbows are regularly stocked, the browns and cutthroats are not, which is added impetus for a successful catch-and-release program.

An hour after sunrise the boat docks at Gaston's, trembling with activity, guides loading up lunches and bait, checking their boats and gear. Above the docks, eager fishermen mingle in the restaurant, drinking one more cup of coffee, wishing each other luck and almost meaning it.

Eight of the big dam's ten generators are on, and the White is up, pale green and running fast. Morning sunlight comes off the surface in wide, bright sheets, as if it were being reflected off polished chrome. The spring wind is cool and steady, the current strong and swift. Our guide for the day is Hank Wilson. Gaston's prides itself on the experience, courtesy, and fishing knowledge of its guides. Wilson has been on the river for nine years.

With the river up and running fast, Wilson quickly maneuvers the john boat into a section of calm water off the right bank protected by a submerged gravel bar and the mouth of a nearby creek. Anchors dropped off the stern and bow keep us steady, parallel to the current. Rods are rigged, reels checked. Wilson, meanwhile, never takes his eyes off the pale-green water. The bottom is clearly visible, a translucent world of stones, swirling moss, and trout, great numbers of them feeding at the edge of the current. "Mostly rainbows," says Wilson, a high trill of excitement in his voice, "and some small cutthroat."

The morning slips by without notice as the day warms and the sun gains the limestone bluffs along the river. Jackets are shed, and the cool wind feels good against the skin. Wilson's sense for where the fish are is incorruptible. Every calm pool boasts another incredible gathering of trout. Farther downriver, we anchor near the mouth of Big Creek, eat ham-and-cheese sandwiches, drink cool sodas, tell fish stories that are only slightly farfetched, and, of course, fish. Up the creek the water warms, and trout give way to the region's splendid and much-sought-after smallmouth bass.

Two- and 3-pounders are common. Although a bass, the smallmouth fights with the determination and tenacity of a trout.

By 4 o'clock we have caught and released twenty-eight trout—all fine fish. The wind comes up, and the surface of the river trembles under its power, producing a steady blue-green chop. The last trout of the day is a big, aggressive rainbow—sleek, supple, heavily muscled. Wilson guesses it weighs at least 5 pounds, maybe more. The fly rod bends under the trout's strength. At the side of the johnboat, a simple pinch of the trout's lip and the hook yields; the trout disappears, a dark shimmering shadow in the deep, green river.

Many excellent fishing camps do business along Arkansas's White and North Fork Rivers. Among the newest is P.J.'s Resort Lodge. Although open for less than three full seasons, P.J.'s is fueled by the same concern for the region's natural beauty and incredible fishing as Gaston's or any of the better fishing camps along these memorable rivers.

With the opening of their lodge, Paul and Joyce Campbell (thus the P and the J of P.J.'s) at long last began to see the realization of a dream that had obsessed them for years, the dream of owning a first-rate fishing lodge on one of the nation's premier trout rivers.

Tall, thin, easy with a smile, Paul Campbell sits tying trout lines in front of a large window that overlooks the White River. He first began thinking of opening a fishing lodge in the early 1970's. A successful businessman in California, Campbell gave up his career to devote himself full time to his painting. Indeed, it was while painting mountain river scenes in the Sierras that he first became obsessed with fly fishing, both as an art and as a lifestyle. Not long afterward, Campbell spent three years criss-crossing the nation, fly fishing all of the country's great trout waters looking for that one unique river, that one truly overpowering place where he would build his lodge and spend the rest of his life. He found that place in the Ozark Mountains of Arkansas. "I came up here by chance," he says smiling broadly, happy at his good fortune. "I remember I caught twenty-two trout in a day here and thinking I would not have to search any farther. The Ozarks was the paradise I was looking for."

The lodge sits in a narrow stretch of the White River Valley just across from the boundary of the Ozark National Forest. While Campbell and his competent staff of angling guides—especially John Gulley, who has been fly fishing these rivers for more than fifteen years, and Bob Snyder—see to the guests' angling needs, Joyce handles the lodge and has already earned a well-deserved reputation as one of the best cooks in the mountains. Even visitors and locals who are not especially interested in angling for trout travel to the lodge to sample Joyce's superb cooking.

Depending on daily weather and water conditions, anglers might find themselves floating the White, wading the North Fork, or taking on the trout of the Little Red, Spring, or Strawberry Rivers. And then there are the trout and smallmouth bass of Big Creek, Mill Creek, the South Fork, and the incredibly beautiful Piney Creek. If the atmosphere of P.J.'s is clothed in one quality, it is comfort, comfort without pretense. The lodge's solitude is embraced rather than enforced.

The last hours of daylight on the North Fork. The water's down, and we have fished all day, stopping only for lunch at Couch's Pit Barbecue in Mountain Home. It's hard to fish these rivers and not stop in at Couch's for a barbecue dinner that is almost as good as the trout fishing.

For an hour now, we have been fishing a riffle that cuts across a gravel bar. On the far side of the riffle is a deep pool shaded by a thicket of overhanging branches. There are brown trout in there by the dozens. As the tiny flies drift naturally on the slow current, the young browns cannot stand it and hit at them every time. Although they are small trout, weighing no more than a pound or two apiece, they are, after all, browns—noble and feisty, belligerent and wild, and each strike is a delight as the low sun flashes hard off the water and the rod bends under their amazing power and strength. And it goes on like this until the sunlight is hardly more than a shadow. Even so, we keep on casting, wanting desperately that this day on the North Fork in the Ozarks might somehow never end.

(1989)

SMOKY MOUNTAINS

Howling Whitewater
in the Soul

Before it is anything else, the Nantahala River is a geometry of sounds rising from the river's steep and narrow mountain gorge filled with a fog of indigo shadows. The headwaters of the Nantahala are mostly in Macon County, North Carolina, and the river tumbles down along the edges of the Indian Springs section of the Nantahala National Forest until it enters Aquone Lake, which the locals call Nantahala Lake.

Below the dam, the river is a series of powerful twists and coils, a frightening and thrilling display of startling hydraulic acrobatics as the river flows toward Fontana Lake, up in the high country of the Great Smoky Mountains, and then onto its junction with the Little Tennessee River.

Well before you see the Nantahala there is its howl, the sound of whitewater, sounds that crackle through the senses like waves of electricity. Boiling up from the ancient, eroded gorge comes a natural symphony of dissonant grumbling, water battered, rent, hissing, roaring, cascading. At a distance, it is like the sound, I imagine, of bowling balls being tossed down a metal staircase. Down along the banks, the river is as pale blue as the mountain shadows and seems in a state of perpetual upheaval, its groan loud and fierce and ceaseless.

Even after all these years of running mountain rivers in canoes and rafts, the sound of whitewater never fails to stir me, jazz the nerves, flood my blood with adrenaline. Suddenly, there is that sharp desire to be on a river again, bucking through runs of whitewater, the turmoil of cascading cold water soaking me, threatening, it always seems, to flood and swamp the raft, suck it down under the cold water in one indifferent gulp.

The southern Appalachian Mountains are laced by such rivers, such water. These ancient mountains hold some of the most haunting, powerful, and beautiful rivers left in the southeast: the Ocoee, Nolichucky, Big South Fork, the rolling Chattooga, the Nantahala, on and on. Each river has its own moods, its own character, its own rhythms. Each is a blend of journey and sojourn, adventure, thrill, and myth. Each is a liquid rite of passage certain to mark in some way all those that travel, mingle with, its waters.

The Nantahala was my first true experience with whitewater. I fell under the river's tempting spell early; though, at first, it wasn't the alluring rapids that obsessed me as much as its population of spooky rainbow trout. And

I keep coming back to the Nantahala, pitching the little blue tent down in the deep gorge, among the shadows and cool drifts of fog, among the galleries of smooth, blue-backed stones.

Not far from where I camp is the now world famous Nantahala Outdoor Center. I can remember when the place opened for business. It was another small mountain enterprise. That was 1972, and the Nantahala Outdoor Center has been taking visitors safely down the Nantahala River ever since. Indeed, these days the center's interests and commitment to the river, to all the earth's wild places, has grown considerably. It travels the world offering customers a vast array of outdoor adventures: back-country cycling and backpacking, a chance to kayak the rivers of Scotland, a journey through the mountains, down the rivers of Nepal.

No matter where the NOC goes, however, each year thousands come to the Nantahala River. They come to feel, no matter how briefly, its unbridled power, its uncorrupted beauty, and of course, the incredible surge of its whitewater. Running the river's rapids is sort of a leap of faith—a moment's connection with the press of the natural world that is worth the crowds, the expense, the raw nerves, the knots of fear in the gut as the first rapid takes hold, claws at the raft, sucks it into a bowl of thwacking waves and clawing currents. For me, running these rapids is not a matter of beating the river, but rather of being a part of it, flowing with it instead of against it.

The old Cherokee name for the Nantahala is Nun-daye-li, Land of the Noonday Sun. A good name and true, because often sunlight does not creep down into the river gorge until well after noon. Another Cherokee name for the river is Shadow River. And it is indeed a place of dancing blue shadows and the haunting wild roar of high mountain rivers, their endlessly cascading whitewater resonating among the mountains like thunder.

(1993)

Pied Piper Casts Spell Upon Pool of Snow

The snow began in the early afternoon. I was fishing a narrow pool of dark water below Proctor's Pool on Hazel Creek, which is on the North Carolina side of Great Smoky Mountains National Park. Standing among a wide gallery of Appalachian greenstones, I worked my fly deep and close, watching the shadows thicken, move heavily among the thick woods along the creek.

As the snow came harder, assaulting the valley in endless white blowing sheets, I hooked a fine, small rainbow trout, quickly brought it close, released it easily. There was no need to touch it. I watched it while it hung for a long moment in the glassy-gray water, the flash of its silvery back, the wide vinaceous smear along its muscled flanks, its incandescent dark eyes. A flick of its tail and it was gone, enveloped by dark water. Not even a ripple of water marked where it had been, so that it seemed as much witch fire as fish.

Moments later, on the far side of the pool, where the gray water went black beneath a great oak half-submerged in the water, I glimpsed a brown trout rising. For an instant, I saw its back, a chaos of mingled color blotch—madder reds glowing in the falling snow like mock suns, then fading, sinking back into the deep water, safe water, water without reflection.

The snow came down harder still, and I climbed out of the creek and hiked upstream to where I had pitched my little blue tent along the bank near Proctor's Pool. In the woods, the snow looked delicate blue, and the entire valley seemed sewn tightly in a membrane of quiet. The only sound was that of the creek, the whispered hiss of fast water moving relentlessly over slick stones.

———◆———

Snow, I always remember, drove Emerson, my grandfather, and my great-uncle Albert, indoors, where the old men would invest their time tying trout flies, an activity that neither of them had a talent for.

Neither do I. My efforts at fly tying always end up looking like evolution's failure. That or some sort of unnatural union of road kill and torched upholstery.

If the old men's attempts at fly tying cared little either for professionalism or tradition, at least their work was constantly interesting, daring, delightfully irreverent. It was never their intention to ape those aquatic and terrestrial insects that had already been more or less successfully imitated. Emerson and Albert were after bigger fare.

Genesis.
Creation.

So when the snow drove them indoors, they would gather around the old desk in the big room whose drawers were stuffed with bits and pieces of calico and felt, gingham and burlap, denim and flannel, gunny and oil-cloth, sackcloth and wools, lengths of colored threads and ribbons, plugs of horse and mule hair, fans of bird feathers, tufts of pile and fuzz, twists of deer fur, hackles of wild turkeys and nervous domestic chickens, musty beaver pelts, and a chaos of shiny buttons.

While the snow whirled outside, the old men would work at the desk. To me, they always looked like bemused minor gods, forsaking reason and good sense, in their search for the great trout concoction, the random mating of fur and feather and colored thread that would break new ground in piscatorial seduction, speak in the language of pure appeal and allure, be the perfect corruption, a deadly hooked bribe, a come-on no trout could refuse, something exotic and completely irresistible.

During a good, long winter storm, the old men could enrich the planet's diversity of creatures by a dozen, all of them scattered about the old desk: abstracts of temptation and motion caught in bizarre twists and wraps of color and flash and texture. There were things with bent wings and no wings, things robust and things obviously gravely wounded, things caught, it seemed to me, either in mid-metamorphosis or mid-metaphor, things gaudy and things humble, things that looked like mutant creatures from another world, and things that looked as innocent as goose down.

The old men's tied trout flies rarely worked, caught fish, until the winter that Albert's hocus-pocus produced a fly that was more fanciful, amorphous, and magical than usual. It was perfectly outlandish and looked, to me, at least, like a harpy in drag.

Emerson and Albert called it the Pied Piper. They baptized it quickly, fishing Starlight Creek in the snow, a delicate blue snow.

The Pied Piper worked.

It still does. It is the old, beat-up fly I caught the fine rainbow trout on below Proctor's Pool, just as it began to snow. It is the fly I caught the brown trout on in a wide dark pool on the South Platte River in Colorado. It was snowing then, too.

Whatever unspoken hypnotic lyric of color and motion the Pied Piper casts, it has something to do with cold mountain streams and a snowfall that looks a delicate blue.

I keep the Pied Piper in a matchbox in my shirt pocket. Emerging from my reverie, thinking of that fine brown trout under the log in dark water, I walked back down to the creek, again tied on the Pied Piper, cast it over the water, let it fall easily on the surface, sink, and tremble through the dark water while whorls of blue snow swirl about me.

(1992)

The Eye's Great Catch

Thin clouds of cold fog drift over the surface of Lake Fontana. I move as sluggishly as a reptile waiting for the sun to warm my blood. Meanwhile, I put my rod and gear in the boat, start the small engine, pull my coat collar high up over my ears before casting off the line. The boat slides easily away from the floating dock and its motor stutters in the cold morning air. Through the wisps of fog I can see the mountains rising high around me. Lake Fontana lies in the Great Smoky Mountains, just across the North Carolina line.

It is fall now, and on this damp morning the bold colors that mark the thick forests look like an artist's palette that has been left out in the heavy dew, the colors moist, rich, running one into the other so that there is, it seems, no clear definition between the reds and oranges, the soft yellows and burnt oranges, the moody browns. High up, the mountains seem on fire, burning with lights that glow but never consume.

Ahead, the lake's surface is as flat and thick as cheap glass. I steer the small boat toward the mouth of Hazel Creek. The wind stings my face, and I dig my free hand deeper into my coat pocket. I am determined not to let the cold break my enthusiasm, erode my longing to see the creek again.

There are hundreds of miles of excellent trout water in these ancient, haggard, uncompromising mountains. Some I have fished once; some many times; but only a few creeks obsess me, flow through me constantly pulling me back at every season.

Hazel Creek is one of these.

Years ago there was an old lumber town along the creek. Name was Proctor. Some say that at one time as many as three thousand people lived along the creek. Although the creek is part of the Great Smoky National Park, each year the park service carries a few people back across the lake to visit the graves of family members. But Proctor is gone; the forest has grown back; the creek and the mountains hang on.

Come spring, I like to backpack to the creek's headwaters, walk down from Clingmans Dome to Silers Bald, spend two or three days enjoying the full-length and many moods of the creek—the cool winds, soft somber shadows, the soothing sound of fast water, moving water rushing over smooth stones, slapping against mammoth granite boulders. But in the fall, I like the bottom reaches of the creek where it widens, gleams in the thin autumn sunlight. It's bucolic in nature, almost pastoral. Too, in the fall, there are fewer people though; despite Hazel Creek's considerable reputation as one of the finest trout streams in the southeast, I have never fished it when I could not find all the solitary water I desired.

There are, I suppose, other creeks in these mountains with more trout, bigger trout. Not far from here flowing through a rugged mountain gap is a big stream where specs (what the natives call brook trout) still thrive above the falls and where an angler can still pursue them without having to crawl on his hands and knees. Within an hour's journey of that creek is another splendid Smoky Mountain trout stream where big browns lurk. Fickle, vexing, and beautiful, their backs a unique deep red, the color of oxblood.

It is not Hazel Creek's trout that haunt me so much as the gentle enticement, the subtle seduction, of its wildness. Thigh-deep in its cold waters, I have known not only memorable trout, but also genuine solitude and solace, the patient trout angler's true rewards.

So I do not mind the cold trip across the lake, for I know what waits at the far shore, at the journey's end.

Fifteen minutes after pulling away from the Fontana resort, the mouth of the creek is in sight, a narrow cove off to the left, and I manage the boat through the shallow water carefully, pulling up the engine prop to avoid submerged rocks.

The sun is just gaining the mountain tops, and shafts of pale sunlight come down the mountainside and fall upon the surface of the creek as if they were liquid. Bursts of light refract off the creek's surface, the light flashing like sparklers. Slowly, without rush, morning creeps down Hazel Creek: shadows flickering on stones; the sound of migrating song birds in the trees; the wind's sigh; and always, the intoxicating sound of swift water.

Trout water.

More than once a nice brown trout has been taken here where the creek empties into the lake. Most anglers tend to dismiss this lower stretch of the creek thinking that such accessible water has probably been overfished.

My experience is otherwise. Fortune and luck treat me well here, and there are always trout, especially in the early months of fall—September and October.

The pack feels good on my back. The weight it holds is no burden; these mountains teach you early to simplify your life, to always travel light. A one-man cocoon tent, down sleeping bag, small backpack stove, food, waders, dry clothes, rain gear, a few other essentials. Nothing more. Barely 40 pounds, if that, including the three travel rods. Nothing that throws anything bigger than a 5-weight line. It is finesse— not power—that raises the trout of Hazel Creek.

Fall flyfishing on Hazel Creek is a time for the experimental, the provocative, the unexpected, the curious, and the improbable. No nail-biting about matching a hatch. Rather, you have to tempt these incorrigible trout, find something that will stir their blood. My collection of dry flies is therefore modest. Some Adams, black gnats, Quill Gordons, Royal Wulffs, mosquitoes. As for nymphs and wet flies, a few McGintys, Parmacheene Belles, Leadwing Coachman, Tellicos, Pheasant Tails, Zug Bugs, hellgrammites, and Gold Ribbed Hare's Ears, all safely tucked away in empty film canisters.

I put up the small blue tent at the Proctor campsite near where a small bend in the creek enters a deep pool of soft-green water. Swift riffles run above and below the pool. The far bank of the pool is undercut, and brush and fallen limbs, even a small tree, hang precariously over the water.

For some months now, each time I have eased up to have a look at Proctor Pool, I have seen the shadow, long, thick, elusive. A great fish is here, or so I have imagined. An old and atavistic trout, cunning, master of this pool as it lies close to the far bank with its hungry jaws pointed upstream.

I do not want to spook such a fine fish, so I have made camp well back from the pool in a small clearing just below the trail that follows the creek up the mountain. I would like to see this fish's impressive shadow again, perhaps raise it into the light, feel the reality of its weight at the end of my line, feel its wildness.

It is almost noon before the tent is up and all the gear arranged, stowed. The sun is already low in the sky, and there is a pleasant wind high among the trees. The rattle of the branches mixes well with the low rush of the creek. Another of Hazel Creek's gifts so freely given: serenity, a serenity that unwrinkles every nerve. I walk upstream along the trail to the wooden foot bridge near the closed ranger's station and fish as the afternoon slips away, peacefully, quietly. I take three rainbow trout in the boulder-strewn section of the creek above the bridge, all with the supple rod and wet flies, two on the McGinty and the last on a Parmacheene Belle. I do not keep the fish. I haven't kept a trout in years. It's not only a matter of conservation, but of choice, a selfish one, I suppose, because I hope that by letting them go, they may again take one of my offerings and haul me out of my world and into theirs.

Daylight begins fading early, withdrawing behind the mountains like an ebbing tide. What light remains along the creek is somber, diaphanous, a tapestry of gently graying shadows. I am already thinking, again, of the big shadow that moves with such grace in the waters of Proctor's Pool.

I switch rods and change flies, retiring the Parmacheene Belle for a No. 12 mosquito dry fly, a temptation of blacks and grays. Perhaps, I think, this is matching, if not a hatch, then at least shadows. I wade down to the pool, so that my position is above and to the right of it as I cast short and let the slow, steady current carry the fly onto the pool's quiet surface. There is not time even to breathe as it rises suddenly from beneath the overhanging branches, rises with the slow caution of a bathysphere, and I watch it rise in that soft gray light. It is powerful, sleek, well over 18 inches in length, and a claret-red streak marks its flanks as it instantly bumps the lingering mosquito with its blunt nose, then disappears again in the deep water becoming once more a beguiling shadow, more image than reality.

Hot chili for supper, eaten under a half moon as I think again of the pool's big trout, a life of power and instinct. I had been too close. The moment it refused the fraudulent mosquito, I caught the glint of my rod in its dark eye.

Tomorrow perhaps, if luck is with me. But, really, it doesn't matter, for I have glimpsed the shadow dissolved, seen the pool's great fish. There are times, I think, when a trout angler must prize what he catches with his eye as highly as what he firmly hooks.

(1991)

Outdoor Medicine

Donner T. McCrady will be 81 this summer. He has a place close to Sugarloaf Mountain near Sylva, North Carolina. When he's not trout fishing or walking up mountain grouse, McCrady keeps a fine garden. There are fresh vegetables most of the year and the sweetest tomatoes in the Smoky Mountains. So says Donner T. McCrady. He claims that tomatoes are the secret to his longevity and excellent health. He eats them every day like apples, only with a dash of salt.

I met McCrady on the Nantahala River precisely five years ago on a splendid June morning at exactly 10:43 AM eastern time.

I remember our meeting in such vivid, crisp detail—not because of McCrady's overwhelming presence but because at precisely 10:41 AM eastern time, I slipped on one of the myriad smooth, slick stones that crowd the Nantahala's channel, and I ended up facedown in the river.

I am an old hand at falling into mountain rivers. It's one of the little inconveniences that plague high-country fly-fishermen. Actually, I have become so adept and skilled at losing my footing in Southern trout streams that these regular blunders often seem like part of my fishing regimen, a sort of aquatic ballet done to add grace and excitement to my cast or perhaps some arcane ritual done intentionally, of course, to rouse some lurking, uncooperative trout.

The fall I took that early-summer morning on the Nantahala was, as I recall, particularly stunning and acrobatic. Even so, I quickly, artfully, casually righted myself, emptied my waders, and made the whole scene seem like part of my normal angling cunning, trout strategy, and all-around stream savvy.

That's when Donner T. McCrady showed up chuckling softly. I ignored him as I worked out my line and secretly hoped my inadvertent plunge had not scared off every trout around. Surely there had to have been at least one old deaf and blind fish in the bunch.

"Quite a tumble," said McCrady. "Yep, these rocks can unsteady a man; it's as if they was coated with grease."

There was a long pause, a scary moment of silence during which I tried to ready myself for what I thought would be the usual offering of wise and useful advice from yet another master angler, the kind I try to steer clear of, the kind who never get wind knots in their line, whose casts are always a blend of skill and art, whose waders never leak, who are as surefooted as goats and never fall into rivers.

Instead, this is what Donner T. McCrady said: "Shoot, guess I've spent most of my life tripping into these mountain rivers. Don't mind, though. Really. I like getting a trout's view of things every once in a while."

I let out a hasty sigh of relief. An honest angler. A kindred spirit. A fellow klutz.

"Oh, by the way," said McCrady, "you're bleeding."

And so I was—a small cut on my right forearm. I noticed McCrady digging hastily through his old wicker creel, yelling he had just the thing to fix me up. A poultice of trout, I thought, as I waded to the stream's edge where McCrady waited.

As it turned out, though, Donner T. McCrady was even a rarer species of outdoorsman than I imagined, a man who fully expects the natural world to get the best of him. His defense: a creel filled not with trout but with medical supplies.

Like a doctor preparing for delicate surgery, McCrady spread the contents of his wicker medical bag on the shady ground beside the river, all the while gently chiding me on my lack of medical preparedness and the importance of keeping even a modest medical kit in one's rucksack when afield.

After all, he went on, the natural world is full of various dangers, potential accidents. Consider his own lifetime of close calls, all occurring in the midst of great beauty and magnificent trout.

Bee stings. Ticks. The inevitable hooked ear and finger and other minor cuts. Twisted ankles. A stunning collection of bumps and bruises. Colds. The flu that dropped him one fall on Chamber's Creek. A smattering of broken bones.

The big brown trout up on Slickrock Creek that bit him savagely. On and on.

Once in the woods, a man just couldn't tell what might befall him, trip him up. Best to pack anticipating every eventuality, including a sudden fever or an attack of catarrh. Better to carry bandages as well as extra socks, ointments as well as a dozen extra dry flies.

So went Donner T. McCrady's First Law of Outdoor Readiness.

The cut on my arm was hardly a scratch, yet spread out on the ground before me were enough medical supplies to treat, I was certain, everything from apoplexy to contact dermatitis.

McCrady smiled broadly, obviously proud of his emergency supplies, his keen sense for disaster, and his medical prowess. "Yep," he said, "I figure I'm ready for just about anything, whether it's frostbite, blisters, or anaphylaxis."

He searched his gear and finally decided that what the cut on my arm called for was a liberal dose of salve and a good-sized adhesive bandage.

"You wouldn't be feeling any chest pain, would you?" McCrady asked considerately, as he rubbed the balm into the cut.

I shook my head.

"Just thought I'd ask. I'm certified in CPR. That's cardiopulmonary resuscitation, you know."

While he tended to the cut, I made a hurried and admiring mental inventory of Donner T. McCrady's basic outdoor medical kit. I thought, "Here indeed is a man suitably prepared."

Percogesic tablets, perhaps twenty adhesive bandages of assorted sizes, chlorpheniramine tablets, antibiotic ointment, meclizine, bacid tablets, gauze pads of various sizes and shapes, butterfly bandages, tape, moleskin, aspirin, snakebite kit, pseudoephedrine tablets, yellow oxide of mercury, dibucaine ointment, bisocodyl tablets, and a Swiss Army knife. Even a small field medical reference manual.

I stared at McCrady's array of medical necessities with genuine wide-eyed wonder. Evidently, I had been leading a precarious, risky, dangerously foolhardy outdoor life, one primed for accident and grief. Perhaps, I thought, there was still enough time to mend my audacious ways, stave off painful misfortune.

I complimented McCrady on his ample medical acumen, thanked him for his help, for the ointment and bandage. I nodded toward his prodigious collection of medical supplies, said I guessed he could handle just about any ailment or condition.

His face went sour.

"Well, not really," he said moodily. "Just be thankful that that spill didn't leave you with a whopping case of the hiccups."

"Hiccups!"

"Yeah. I'm fresh out of peanut butter."

These days, thanks to the example of Donner T. McCrady, I always try to carry some kind of medical kit when I'm afield, even if it's only a couple of aspirin and a slip of paper with my insurance company's telephone number on it. Peace of mind is worth the effort.

As McCrady says, "Fishing for trout is trouble enough. Why ask for more."

(1989)

High-Country Trout

The scene could unfold anywhere, really. In the fast-water, high-country trout streams of a half-dozen Southern states. Perhaps it is early morning in the chilly waters of Arkansas' White River, anglers standing thigh deep in the river, half hidden by the perpetual mist that hangs over the river year-round like clouds of smoky fog. Maybe it is on one of West Virginia's many fine trout streams, perhaps Wolf Creek or Laurel Fork, both of which are part of the magnificent Cheat River system. Certainly, it could be along the hundreds of first-class Virginia trout streams, streams like the Bullpasture, which when once fished are never forgotten but become a permanent part of the fly-fisherman's litany of rivers fished and trout caught. There are more than 2,000 miles of excellent trout fishing in the creeks and streams of North Georgia, but it is in North Carolina and Tennessee that the trout run thickest. In these two states alone there are more than four-thousand trout streams.

Across the South's high country on almost any spring morning, the fly-fishermen come with their lithe, willowy rods and supple line and their delicate artificial flies. Of course, they come for trout. But there is more to fly fishing than fish. They come, too, for the mountains' solace and for the streams' swift waters and endless comfort. They come for the solitude. Fly fishing is as much a piscatorial pilgrimage as it is a mere contest between man and trout.

Trout, fly fishing, and high-mountain streams are inexorably interwoven. There is something inexplicable about mountain trout. Perhaps it is their untamed, unbroken character. Whatever the allure, they pull on the fisherman with unbridled passion.

Each year, at any of a thousand Southern mountain streams, the same ritual begins anew. Wearing patched waders, a man will stand downstream from some handsome pool or riffle and cast line and fly above it, letting his fraudulent offering drift on the surface. One cast. Two. Nothing. Then on the third cast it happens. Curiosity bites. The slim graphite rod bends as the angler jerks rod and line straight up in the air. The trout surfaces and leaps. It is a rainbow trout, perhaps 2 pounds. There is a smudge of red along its lateral line that looks like strawberry jam. It leaps again and glistens in the early-morning light. Slowly, the angler pulls this handsome fish to his landing net, where he carefully removes the hook. Many fly-fishermen prefer to release their fish. It is a personal decision. Some fly-fishermen mount trout on their walls; others mount them in their imaginations.

For a long time anglers have tended to snub Southern trout. Attitudes change, however, and today in the South, fly fishing is enjoying a renaissance as anglers rediscover its simplicity, grace, rich heritage, intellectual challenge, and slightly mystical allure.

While a great many Southern states enjoy some truly excellent trout fishing, the streams of the Smoky Mountains hold what is perhaps some of the region's most rugged, pristine, and spectacular fly-fishing waters. In these mountains even the most implacable fly-fisherman could easily fish a lifetime and only begin to sample the bounty of the Smoky Mountain streams.

Separating North Carolina and Tennessee, the Smoky Mountains, as part of the Appalachian chain, are some of the earth's oldest mountains. Within these rough mountains, thirteen major watersheds feed hundreds of miles of fast-running, clean, cold streams—almost all of them full of trout. Many of the better streams fall within the huge Smoky Mountains National Park, which covers a half-million acres of high country in North Carolina and Tennessee. As many as six to eight million visitors snake through the park each year. Despite such intimidating figures, fly-fishermen on the park's streams can fish for days without seeing another person or feeling the press of the outside world.

These mountain rivers are rich in life. Some support as many as sixty-five different species of fish. Fly-fishermen, however, are interested in only three—the brook trout, rainbow trout, and brown trout. Increasingly rare and threatened, the beautiful and elusive brook trout is the only true native of Southern highland mountain streams. Rainbows and browns are immigrants, but in the national park streams they are essentially wild because these streams have not been stocked for years. Actually, the brook trout is not a true trout at all, but a char. Among fly-fishermen, though, such distinctions are left to ichthyologists. Once abundant, the beautifully colored brook trout is now in trouble throughout most of its range. In 1975 officials at the Smoky Mountain National Park placed a moratorium on brook trout fishing. Where it is not closed altogether, only catch-and-release brook trout fishing is permitted.

While the brook trout population struggles, rainbows and browns are thriving, not only in the Smokies but in most high-mountain Southern trout streams as well. In the park and elsewhere, rainbows are now the dominant Southern trout, although the browns are an aggressive trout and are already competing with rainbows for territory. In character, brown trout are moody and unpredictable, while rainbows are relished for a fighting spirit that far exceeds their size.

Rainbows were first stocked in Smoky Mountain streams in the early 1900s. They adapted quickly, and today a good high-country rainbow can run up to 4 pounds and measure more than 10 inches. Rainbows are fearless and have healthy appetites. There is little that is selective about their eating habits. They are scavengers and will dine on whatever is at hand.

Brown trout are bigger, more elusive, vexing. Some taken inside the park have weighed in at more than 10 pounds. Shy, even secretive, they are an uncanny fish. Ten minutes with one hooked on a dry fly and a thin tippet on a lightweight rod is roughly comparable to trying to haul in a tarpon with dental floss.

Southern trout streams differ in character. Each one shoulders a variety of moods. Even so, in the high country of the Smokies, many of the better trout streams are oxygen rich and rather acidic. Although they do occur, regular insect hatches are sporadic. Such conditions have made the trout wide ranging feeders. This, in turn, gives the fly-fisherman more latitude in the artificial flies he can use with success. Conditions change constantly on any trout stream, and it is these conditions that will help determine what artificial fly the angler chooses to tie on his line.

When it comes to matters of flies and other gear, fly-fishermen are extremely eclectic. Tastes differ. However, for most high-mountain Southern streams, fly-fishermen prefer the shorter graphite rods, something between 6.75 and 8.5 feet. These rods are especially good on smaller streams that restrict casting. Likewise, smaller line sizes work best in the South—anything from the spidery, delicate, nearly translucent No.2 to the heavier No.5. Southern fly-fishermen generally like to work with longer leaders, too, which allows them greater opportunity to sneak up on wary trout. On Southern streams, from the North River in Virginia to the Georgia/South Carolina portion of the roaring Chattooga, it is not uncommon to see a savvy fly-fisherman casting with at least 20 feet of leader. Sometimes this is the only means of tempting a fat rainbow sunk beneath a log in a pool of flat, still water as clear as a glass of gin.

A Southern fly-fisherman's fly box, once opened, generally looks like an artist's palette that has been dipped in water: it is a collage of brilliant colors. Whatever else he carries with him, though, the Southern fly-fisherman, especially if he fishes for high-mountain trout, will have these on hand: the Yallarhammar, an effective local Smoky Mountain fly; a half-dozen Adams and Wulffs (sizes 10-16); several Royal Coachman flies (sizes 10-14); the indispensable Tellico nymph, perhaps the best all-season fly for the Smokies; some brown Elkwings and stoneflies (black and yellow, sizes 10-14); and plenty of terrestrials (imitations of land insects), including Letort hoppers, black and cinnamon ants, and a handful of Irresistibles (sizes 10-16).

Gear assembled, time allotted, there remains for the fly-fisherman in the Smokies one last great difficulty—where to fish. There are excellent streams scattered throughout the park and beyond its boundaries as well. On the far side of the park, near Bryson City, North Carolina, there are what many Southern fly-fishermen consider the two best trout streams in the Smokies: Deep Creek and Hazel Creek. There are primitive campsites on both creeks so anglers can completely immerse themselves in the mountains, become a part of them for days on end. Nearby are Fontana and the delightful finger lakes of the Smokies—Cheoah, Calderwood, and Chilhowee—also known for their big trout. There is even a cherished belief that descendants of the steelhead (or migrating rainbows) stocked long ago still run in these lakes.

Of course, there is superb trout fishing near Gatlinburg, Cherokee, and Townsend. Gatlinburg puts the angler close to such streams as the Little Pigeon, Little River, and the revered Abrams Creek at Cades Cove. Too, the Greenbriar River, another fine trout stream, is also within driving distance of Gatlinburg. Cherokee puts the fly-fisherman near more excellent water, including Collins Creek, Raven

Fork, and Soco Creek. Oualla Indian Reservation daily fishing licenses can be purchased in Cherokee.

Anglers staying at the Fontana Village Resort on Fontana Lake have access to Hazel Creek, Eagle Creek, Chambers, and Forney Creek. Cosby is another popular base camp for fly-fishermen in the Smokies. It puts them close to the Middle Prong of the Little Pigeon, the Greenbriar, the West Prong of the Little Pigeon, Deep Creek, and naturally, Little Cosby Creek. The one other premier Smoky Mountains trout stream is the almost pastoral Cataloochee Creek.

Unlike a deep-sea angler, the mountain fly-fisherman is not an angler of long journeys. He likes the mountain streams and the trout within them. His accolades come not from big fish, but from the angling life and all that it entails. Fly fishing in the high-mountain South is not just a sport, it is a way of life. The fly-fisherman comes to a mountain stream and knows it as he knows a good friend. With loops of line over its shiny surface, he stitches together a lifetime of fast water and irrepressible trout.

(1988)

A Haunting Obsession with the Brown Trout

The days seem an endless press of short, violent tropical thunderstorms followed by steamy storm-tossed skies, brooding blue-black clouds, and yet, more rain. All in all, it is weather that leaches the spirit as well as bones, muscles, and nerves.

As the rains claw at my window here in Alabama, I find myself thinking of the high country to the north, the Great Smoky Mountains, the cool wind and chilly shadows up above 3,000 feet, the wonderful feel of mountain rivers, cold and fast, cascading down through narrow, pinched-in valleys, splashing over the slick backs of gray-green Appalachian greenstone.

There are trout in those rivers, wild and uncompromising as the waters they live in. As a confessed junkie for wild rivers and wild trout, I've tried to keep my addiction inclusive rather than exclusive, but I admit that it is brown trout that haunt me most of all.

While I love them all, I'm obsessed with brown trout, perhaps because the first trout I caught, when I was a boy, was a brown trout. I hooked it and it hooked me. Come to think of it, the last trout I caught, in a deep blue-green pool of bright water on the Middle Fork of the South Platte River in Colorado, was a brown trout. It was a big brown. I hooked it three times, and three times it threw the fly and hook, broke my spidery tippet.

Some fish.

Brown trout, *Salmo trutta*. Stout, fusiform, the brown trout is the nearly perfect expression of practical, piscine elegance and efficiency. A trout with an attitude. A survivor that isn't sensitive about what it has to do to survive. Fierce and slack-jawed, its double rows of teeth allow it to be ecumenical when it comes to diet. It will eat another trout with the same relish as it will eat the occasional small rodent fortune sends down a river.

Brown trout can tolerate, not only hang on but thrive, in a greater diversity of water conditions than most trout. Consequently, brown trout have been introduced successfully wherever suitable water conditions exist and now can be found from North America to New Zealand, even parts of Asia and Africa.

Like me, like most of us, the brown trout is not a native American. It got here not by evolving through time in the primal blue waters, but aboard the ocean liner Werra. When the liner docked in New York City from Germany in the early 1880s, among its passengers were eight-thousand brown trout eggs, carefully packed and chilled.

The eggs were a gift from Lucius von Behr to Fred Mather, an American angler and writer who ran a fish hatchery on Long Island. The two men met and became friends at the International Fisheries Exposition in Berlin. Most of the brown trout eggs aboard the Werra went to Mather's Long Island fish hatchery. The rest were sent north and west to Michigan, where the survivors were eventually released in the Pere Marquette River, which became America's first brown trout river. These German brown trout were later joined with their black-spotted cousins from Scotland, the Loch Leven brown trout, and in no time the brown trout was introduced into the trout waters of more than thirty states.

It is the brown trout of Slickrock Creek in the Great Smoky Mountains that I spend these long summer days dreaming about. Slickrock browns carry the creek and the mountains on their flanks and backs and bellies, a geography of form and color, shadow and light and motion. They are a blend of olive greens and the warm golds of melted honey marked by a chaos of dark, irregular spots or splotches along the flanks and back, even the squared tail, and often these black starbursts are edged with thin halos of amber and burnt orange, sulphur yellow. Sometimes their bone-white bellies are fringed in yellow, as though delicately dipped in butter.

As the rain falls, I keep thinking about the creek, the brown trout in the deep water, down among black stones and dark water, how when they rise their backs look like a blood-red sun spilling over the edges of a black sea.

(1992)

DAYS
AFIELD

Giving Thanks

It's April, and everywhere in these Southern mountains there is new growth, vibrant color taking hold all along the weathered ridges. At first light the hills are a wash of greens—shiny holly greens; softer, deeper emerald greens, especially where the old homesteads once stood; subtler olive greens and pale yellow greens in the hollows where the shadows linger. April: the verdant month.

The morning wind is light and chilly, blowing out of the south and feathering to the west. A good turkey wind, at least in these Appalachian Mountains. Deep in the shadows that ease among the trees like a black fog, cardinals sing. Down below Hagger's Cove, just at daybreak, a barred owl hoots, a bold protest against the building light. Instantly, a wild gobbler answers, drowning the owl's call in a loud, belligerent tide of discordant invective.

The owl's call and the old wild turkey's immediate and bellicose response, more of a challenge than a call, set my course. Judging from the sound, the turkey seems to be among a stand of oaks above the cove along the ridge, not far from an abandoned orchard.

I move north, staying out of the wind, easing over boulders and through the cold waters of Turner's Falls, holding the old Winchester 12-gauge pump shotgun high overhead. The creek dropping along the cove is still in inky shadows, and there are slick moss-covered stones and sudden sinkholes everywhere along its course, patiently waiting to swallow up even the most innocent of intruders. There is an urgency to the tug of mountain streams, a reminder that every journey into these mountains is one of significance, whether it is hiking a trail, pursuing a wild turkey, or just resting beside a stream. Crossing Turner's Falls I think of how many springs I have come into these mountains, each trip a search not only for wild turkeys but also for the new season itself. But the years, like the waters of Turner's Falls, mingle inexorably and are inseparable, run in the memory and imagination as one season, the early-morning hours punctuated by the caterwauling of the wild turkey.

The thin morning light presses against the mountain shadows the way waves press against the shore—relentlessly. As the sunlight intensifies, the barred owl in the cove settles into silence. Mimicking its call, I let loose an owling sound. Still up on the ridge, the gobbler greets my call with fitting disdain and irritation. Wild turkeys cannot abide owls. The turkey's response is as instantaneous as an avalanche. Come early spring, the wild turkey seems to be these mountains' voice, one making no promises but rather hinting at possibilities.

Above, the ridge line shakes off the last of the morning; even the dew has evaporated. I move on, deciding to head slightly north of true east, hoping to stay in the shadows, the wind to my face. This is not wild turkey strategy. Any man who fools around with wild turkeys long enough comes to know, at last, there is really no such thing as a strategy when dealing with such a perplexing creature. There is only a good lunch and a necessary trust in good fortune. Mother luck.

Walking another 60 paces, I stop behind the soothing shadow of a hickory tree and let out another fraudulent barred owl call up toward the ridge line. This time the turkey's reaction is shorter, curt, muffled, as if it had other matters on its mind besides quarrelsome owls. Now, certainly, it has come down from its roost, is on the ground. Perhaps it is feeding. More likely, it is moving slowly and nervously looking for available hens.

Suddenly, every leaf and twig, every loose stone, any sudden and unnatural noise, is a conspirator, eager to give away my presence. A squirrel's nagging bark, a crow's nasty squawk, a bird's startled cry—anything out of the ordinary will alert a turkey, cause it to disappear as though it were a thin morning mist. Wild turkeys are suspicious creatures, uncertain of everything, a bird given to illogical and unreasonable fits and starts. It survives because it trusts few things, not even, at times, its own instincts.

Working my way as quietly yet as quickly as I can up toward the ridge, I finally settle on the east side of a big oak facing the abandoned farm orchard. Gnarled apple trees, their limbs bent like arthritic fingers, still mark the old orchard. Under the trees, a small meadow of mountain wildflowers is in bloom. The big oak casts a fine shadow over me. I am enveloped in a thick charcoal-colored light. The Winchester is across my lap as I take the yellowed turkey wingbone from my pocket, yelp, once, twice, three times, trying to make the sound not so much original as candid, brash, exciting, tempting. A minute passes. Then five. Another gentle yelp, more purring in tone, not loud or overeager. It comes then, takes shape at the far edge of the orchard, eases out of the shadows and tangled shrubs perhaps 80 paces from the oak tree. At first, only its head is visible. As big as a baseball, this turkey's head is a mix of colors that anywhere else would suggest bad modern art—smudges of cadet blue, lobster reds, dabs of grizzled white, and a dark, nervous eye measuring every detail of the world about it.

It is a handsome bird, though, as it at last carefully moves into the small meadow, into full view: wattles thick, swollen oxblood red, and a single ragged beard dangling from its powerful chest. From the length of the beard (perhaps 11 inches), the bird's size, and the size of its spurs, I guess that this turkey is well past its second year.

Sitting there against the oak, I wonder for a moment if there might be a word that will embrace the wild turkey. Motion, perhaps. Cautious motion. The turkey in the meadow, like all its kind, never stops moving completely, never stops surveying every inch of ground, every gust of wind. Unpredictable motion: Just when I think it has caught sight of me, it prances to within 70 paces of my hiding place in the oak's shadow and begins to strut. Such a bold ego, such assurance, its body puffed out, wings vigorously dusting the ground, kicking up grass and dirt and wildflowers as it plays its courtier's ace, the glorious spread of its tail feathers as it holds its head and neck tight against its swollen chest. In the morning light, its feathers are iridescent, a moving pool of flashing colors. On and on the dance goes, an ancient spring ritual played out on this morning in a long-abandoned homestead meadow under apple trees.

Even so, a heady affair, and I forget myself and decide against shouldering the Winchester. On this morning it is enough just to sit here in the cool shade and watch, a hidden spectator to one of the natural world's most intriguing and delightful celebrations. I watch until the old gobbler finally realizes that its efforts have drawn no hen's attention. The old bird straightens up, shakes its heavy body forcefully, throws one last glance at the orchard like a lover suddenly realizing he's been made the fool—and then moves off toward the woods' edge, its head high and unrepentant.

I sit by the oak for a while longer, letting the sun burn away the last of the long, thin shadows. Wild turkeys, of course, are mostly thought of, by everyone except turkey hunters that is, in the fall. November: the grand symbol of Thanksgiving, of bounty, rich harvests, survival. "See a wild turkey," my great-uncle said, "and count your blessings." And I know that that is as true in April as it is in November. I take a hardboiled egg from my coat pocket, peel it, drink cool well water from my canteen. A splendid Thanksgiving meal, no matter the season, especially if you have just spent a morning in the mountains watching a wild turkey strut for a moment not long after dawn, the sunlight flashing off its back as though its feathers have been dipped in molten copper.

(1989)

No Deer

Come winter, when the Atchafalaya swamp is damp and cold, drenched with dew and fog, my neighbor William Turlow and I go into the swamp determined to lessen Louisiana's deer population by at least one.

This winter was one of my finest as a hunter, yet I did not shoot a thing. During these winter expeditions, Turlow and I like to call ourselves hunters, but actually we are hardly that. Other than these few weeks in the winter woods, most of our killing is done on the farm. Neither of us is much of a shot.

But on the last Saturday of December we always go into the swamp looking for a deer. This year we met at dawn, the moon still bright in the sky; had coffee and bacon while we checked our gear and supplies; then set out toward the thick, dark woods beyond Krotz Springs. The moon washed the highway in a light as white as lilacs. It had been raining before the moon broke clear of the sky's heavy net of tendril clouds. The rain had been cold, steady but not brutal, and now mist hung low over the beanfields like streamers of lace. We left the 1947 blue Willis at the edge of a fallow field and walked toward the thin willows at the swamp's edge. Turlow walked ahead, his well-worn Browning shotgun tucked under his arm and a gray fedora pulled down tight on his head. Among the hunters, trappers, and storytellers of the Atchafalaya basin, Turlow is a man of considerable importance, for he knows where deer cross the marsh looking for stands of fresh dewberry, their favorite browse. Ahead of Turlow, 2 miles to the east, the swamp is lush, heady with the smell of old summer and autumn, of mold and rot.

Slowly the woods filled with the sounds of sunrise: a water thrush scuttling among the low brush, barred owls barking from the cypress trees, the gentle thud of dew hitting the forest floor, the cries of crows everywhere. I put on an orange vest and hunter's cap to warn whatever other hunters there might be in the swamp that I would look awfully silly strapped across the hood of some pickup truck. In the woods, the distinctions are clearly drawn: deer, clothed in white tails and fur the color of new chestnuts, are all speed and grace; hunters, cold and hungry, dressed in blazing orange, dream of deer flashing through the marsh, throwing shadows across the low morning sun.

Where the hardwoods thinned to clumps, I shinnied up a small willow, crouched between limb and trunk, and began my vigil. No deer came. Or if any were around, they were not showing themselves, at least not to anyone wearing orange. The sun climbed higher and steam rose from the woods like smoke. Turlow pushed back his gray fedora and shrugged his broad shoulders. As the morning wore on, I gladly gave in to idle diversions. I ate more bacon, watched fish crows drift easily from slough to slough looking for an easy meal, dreamed, and dozed. Still, no deer came. Suddenly the morning's murmurs gave way to a symphony of wings. Overhead, rafts of duck were strung across the sky in shoelace formations. Some of the birds flew close to the trees; others seemed determined to fly into the sun. There were pintails and mallards, some bluebills, mergansers, and green wing teal. Magnificent and thrilling, the sight gave the morning new excitement and promise. The woods shuddered with the ducks' deep-throated rasping. So many were there that for a time they blocked the sun. And still no deer came.

I gave up my notch in the willow, came down to earth, took off my vest, lowered my colors. This morning, at least, the deer had found another place to cross the marsh, somewhere more to their liking, perhaps less crowded. Maybe it is best, after all, if the spot where deer cross a wood stays a mystery. It is enough just to be here, whether the deer come or not.

I stretched under the willow, a deerslayer unarmed, content to eat hardboiled eggs and watch red-tailed hawks ride the building thermals. Turlow traded his rifle for a fishing pole fashioned from a scrub oak limb and baited it with bits of his cheese sandwich. He made no excuses for missing the deer. As he had said before, the swamp makes no promises; it offers surprises, not guarantees. This is part of its beauty and allure.

I had never completely understood why I liked to hunt, to get into the woods. On this winter morning, when no deer appeared, I began to understand at least this much: not all hunting has much to do with putting an animal between the crosshairs. It has to do with a way of life lost and found, of time and place, of history, of beginnings and endings, and too, of constancy.

At day's end the red-tailed hawk came again, low to the ground, casting his great shadow over Turlow and the fishing pole, over me, over the wood.

(1982)

Camp Cook

No one knows how John Ellis got to be camp cook of the Half Moon Hunting and Fishing Club, though the prevailing suspicion is that he assumed the post naturally because he is the only club member who regularly remembers the salt, a can opener, and paper plates. John Ellis can also name, without outside assistance, at least two of the four basic food groups, and he knows that a ladle is not a new attachment for gas-operated shotguns.

John Ellis is a Cajun and an outdoor cook who dearly loves his work and often can be found at the camp sitting out by a hickory wood fire in the cold November moonlight, reading through the latest issues of *Good Housekeeping* and *Gourmet* magazines, clipping out appealing recipes, keeping his eye open for interesting and fun things to do with squirrel and tartar sauce and venison casseroles.

This year, on a bright and chilly day in October, John Ellis showed up at the camp at the edge of Hog Bayou the way he always shows up, looking like a rumpled old peddler loaded down with Browning rifles and shotguns, suitcase, and two old Army-green duffle bags. In one he carries an assortment of shells and socks, toothbrush and tooth paste; in the other he carries his pots and pans, herbs and spices, napkins and corkscrew.

The question of food is a touchy one with any hunting club. Generally, outdoorsmen are hearty and dedicated eaters as long as they don't have to do the cooking. The charter of the Half Moon Hunting and Fishing Club mentions nothing about cooking and says only that "each member will provide some kind of food." As a matter of tradition, whatever food is brought cannot make noises, be wrapped in old clothing, or be any shade of green. John Ellis, periodically slapping his thigh with a wooden serving spoon, oversees the stockpiling of provisions in the corner of the camp by the Coleman stove. Each contribution is carefully noted and assigned a place in the kitchen by John Ellis. This season, for instance, Willard McRoy, a man who believes steadfastly in never hunting anything before ten o'clock in the morning, brought an ice chest full of baloney, cheese, onion dip, seven packages of potato chips, and a case of root beer. McRoy believes that everything is edible.

"What? No rhubarb surprise this year, Willard?" snapped John Ellis.

Believing that when a man goes into the woods he ought to live like a true frontiersman, Clarence Lee showed up with his usual allotment of beef jerky and tap water.

"Somebody check Clarence Lee's gear for stashed Baby Ruths and Moon Pies," sneered John Ellis. "Let's not forget last season's nasty little incident when Clarence Lee spent half his time with the game warden trying to trade duck feathers for peanut butter and jelly sandwiches."

Wilfred Bates, a divorced tree surgeon, checked in with pimento and cheese spread and a box of crackers, and sad-eyed Ogden brought breakfast—two dozen Egg McMuffins and a quart of V-8 juice.

To this odd assortment of groceries John Ellis plied his usual culinary magic. Hot pad in hand, he is all of a sudden a bearded Julia Child dressed in a blue and red ski suit, a white handkerchief tied about his waist for an apron, whistling John Phillip Sousa marches and smelling of bug dope. Among those who have survived it, John Ellis's stew is legendary, if not lethal. While he is a modest man and generally shies away from talking about himself or his cooking, when pressed, John Ellis proudly credits his stew's rich and enduring flavor mostly to the garlic and pepper and to the fact that he no longer picks the bugs out of it.

"Bugs are always landing in the pot. Mostly, its mosquitoes or an occasional beetle. They get bogged down, like a man in the swamp after a heavy autumn rain. I got tired of having to fish 'em out, so a couple of years ago I gave up trying and just started stirring them in. What harm are a couple of mosquitoes, beetles, and moths, after all?" says John Ellis firmly, a broad smile on his face.

Last Friday evening Clarence Lee and I were out in Big Bayou creeping cat squirrels when we first noticed it: a curious odor on the wind coating every tree and leaf like wood smoke. At the time, Clarence Lee was trading insults with a barking squirrel up in a big hickory near Duck Bayou.

"What'ya make of it," said Clarence Lee, his nose twitching, his face suddenly drained of color, his eyes swimming in panic.

"He's some squirrel," I said.

"No, no, that smell," screamed Clarence Lee, "that smell!"

He quickly reached inside his vest pocket, pulled out a map wrapped carefully in a zip-lock plastic bag. This was no ordinary map, for on it Clarence Lee had meticulously noted with a dark felt pen the quickest escape routes from the camp and highlighted every restaurant, fast-food place, snack bar, supermarket, and roadside eatery within twenty miles.

All of a sudden, the wind changed direction, blew now from the northeast, and the strange odor began to form dense, heavy clouds among the oaks and willows, in the low sloughs and bayous. What seemed to be low groanings were heard coming from the direction of the camp.

"Forest fire!," yelled Clarence Lee as he was slowly enveloped by the thick smoke.

"No," I said. "It smells more like scorched rice or two-month-old milk. Maybe Bates finally got the skunk that has been stealing the grapes he has hidden under his cot. Wait a minute. This is Friday. Maybe it is John Ellis's pork chop soup."

Clarence Lee and I regarded each other closely.

"According to my map and compass," Clarence Lee said desperately, "there is an A&P supermarket a mile east of the river."

"Think of it," shouted Clarence Lee as we raced toward the river. "Spam. Vienna Sausage and crackers. Peanut butter and jelly. Real Food!"

(1985)

Ruffed Grouse:
The Highlands' Noble Bird

Sometime during the night, fog seeped down the Virginia mountainsides with the suddenness of an avalanche and spread quietly over the valley, covering it like a quilt. Now, at dawn, above the fog, sunlight flashes, sparkles on the fast-moving waters of the mountain streams. Autumn's dramatic colors glow intensely from every slope and form a tapestry of bold reds, soothing yellows, soft oranges, and subtle browns.

Rachael, an English setter, sits near the tailgate pounding the truck bed with her black-and-white spotted tail. She is a beautiful dog, with thick fur as fine as a beaver pelt. We park the truck on a little-used forest trail. Bob, Rachael's owner, fastens a collar with a small bell on it around her neck and lets her out. On the run, she sounds like a circuit preacher trying to ring in his far-flung congregation.

The morning wind, out of the southwest, is light and cool, and there is nothing on our minds but these mountains and the grouse among them, as elusive as dreams.

Southerners' love affair with grouse is an old and sweet one, going back to when their ancestors first settled these rugged mountains. Grouse and grouse hunting are an intrinsic part of their lives and common heritage, as natural as breathing. And to the grouse hunter, there is no other bird as imposing and venerable, as challenging or vexing as the grouse. After all, you do not hunt grouse as much as you seek them out. The ultimate reward is not in shooting them but in merely finding them. The hunt is a convenient excuse to walk these splendid mountains behind a tireless dog as intoxicated by the woods as you are, and to participate in an ageless adventure that is still sharp and intriguing and endlessly gratifying.

There is nothing easy about grouse, and not every upland bird hunter extols them. After all, they hang out in the most rugged and exhausting terrain that thoroughly tests a hunter's skill, conditioning, and resolve. Hunting grouse is hard work, trying at best, grueling at worst. Even when found, grouse prove to be the most unpredictable of birds, both on the ground and in flight. A bird hunter can really never figure out a grouse the way he can a quail or a pheasant. The grouse's character is like that of a wild turkey—suspicious, jumpy, distrustful, and totally uncooperative. Thankfully, they never seem to act the way science and good sense dictate.

Bob shoulders his Remington 20 gauge; I decide on my little 16 gauge. The major difference between grouse hunters and other upland bird hunters is that grouse hunters tend to be a far more humble bunch because, if there's anything more difficult than finding a grouse, it's shooting one. Truly, if grouse hunters have a soulmate, it's the angler. Both dedicate a lot of their time to stories and dreams of the one that got away.

Rachael's bell tells us that she is working a laurel thicket just up the hillside. Above us is the rushing sound of Tavern Creek. The countryside has more folds to it than an accordion. Rachael is tireless and works her way through dense pockets of woods and laurel thickets, tangled labyrinths of wild grapevines and unyielding walls of rhododendron. Then we hear it. Quiet. Except for the creek's swift waters, Rachael's bell no longer tolls. Somewhere in the silence, hopefully, crouches a grouse exquisitely concealed and camouflaged, no more recognizable than one leaf in a thousand identical leaves.

Rachael stands half enveloped in a clump of laurel, her body bent in an exaggerated arch. Her head is down and tilted slightly to the left. We catch just a glimpse of the ruffed grouse, a wise tactician, winging its way between oak branches and then over the hill. We had witnessed such flights before, hundreds of times, and the astonishment and thrill of the moment never fades, dulls, or dissipates. It is always a wonder.

Navigating by Rachael's tail, Bob and I walk, observe, talk in low voices. The conversation never changes: Grouse are birds of consequence. More handsome than flamboyant, grouse wear the wood's colors, hues of the earth, mottled browns, speckled grays, flat blacks, dull whites fashioned in patterns resembling lichen on gray stones. The head is that of an aristocrat topped by an uneven crest reminiscent of a Mohawk haircut. The squared tail, when flaired, suggests a ceremonial fan. Grouse survive, even thrive, because they are synonymous with their habitat, indistinguishable from other gatherings of downed twigs, leaves, knot of thorns, or loose stones. "It's like hunting ghosts," laments Bob.

Grouse like the comfort and security of the forest floor; though when startled or threatened, they can be, to every hunter's chagrin, deceptively swift and acrobatic fliers. Grouse feed mostly on insects, buds, and berries, which helps explain their exasperating fondness for honeysuckle, laurel, and rhododendron thickets. They like to forage in the early morning and again just before dusk. During the long hours of daylight, they rest in the shadows, making few movements or sounds, and leaving little scent. Unless the birds are moving or have just settled down, even a good grouse dog has difficulty finding them.

By midmorning we have actually seen two grouse and heard, we think, three more. Neither of us has fired a shot. So far, a good day. Bob is especially content, happy that grouse still hang on in these Virginia hills. Even though grouse hunters are on the increase, the birds continue to do well. Development of these mountains, not the nervous grouse hunters, is the birds' greatest adversary, natural or otherwise. Populations remain healthy and constant throughout a great portion of the northern reaches of the Appalachians, especially in parts of North Carolina, Virginia, West Virginia, and Maryland.

Rachael leads us along a creekbed under huge hardwoods where it is cool and the sunlight thins, almost threatens to dissolve. Searching for grouse involves a journey not simply through these mountains, but into them. Details become clearer, sharper. Every sound, motion, and smell is greatly intensified. Each step we take leads to the unexpected. Again, Rachael's bell falls silent. We freeze. The wind rattles dead oak leaves. Bob walks ahead, shotgun ready. The flushed grouse zooms over Bob's left shoulder. He swings, fires, misses. A difficult shot, as are most grouse shots.

At the other end of the same thicket, Rachael smells more aggravation. She stops suddenly, ringing the bell once. This time Bob is right behind her, less than a foot from her tail. He takes a giant gulp of air to settle his composure, moves ahead. The bird holds tight, another attribute of grouse, and doesn't flush until Bob has passed it. Pivoting, Bob levels the dark-barreled Remington and intercepts the low buzzing bolt of feathered electricity. One for the skillet.

It is nearly noon. The day's bounty will yield another grouse up by Miller's Ford. We do not get back to the truck until dusk, our excitement intact but our bodies exhausted—although Rachael cannot quite understand why we're giving up so soon. We drive down the mountain, along the edge of the valley. Below, the houses of the town are strung out through the narrow valley like a gleaming string of Christmas lights.

(1988)

Hard Winters and
Crazy Birds

The day was so cold time itself seemed nearly frozen. The hours moved with an icy apathy. Meanwhile, the news on the radio called for more of the same. There was a cold front plodding steadily down from Kansas and Colorado, bringing a cold that would be deep and wide and sit heavily on the land, the kind of numbing cold that brought a cheerful smile to Grady Moorfield's ruddy face.

"Hear that? Cold front's coming," he said. "Birds will be moving, certain as thunder after lightning."

Moorfield got up from his chair and looked out the kitchen window past spent fields of corn and beans, out toward the creek bottom full of dull winter light and choked by tangles of saplings and honeysuckle, labyrinths of greenbrier and wild grapevines and cane. The innocent smile on Moorfield's face began to widen.

"It's a good sign," he said, his back to me. "A cold snap like this will put 'em in the air all right, push 'em south, bring 'em this way. Late tomorrow, maybe. Next day for sure, and the creek bottom will be full of 'em, enough to get my old blood to moving again. Wood snipe. Just the thought of 'em makes me nervous."

A moment now for names. Even among truly bizarre birds, including wild turkeys and common crows, woodcock seem particularly outrageous, even nonsensical. Indeed, their often-preposterous behavior is perhaps their most endearing characteristic. A man hopelessly entangled in an alder thicket on an icy winter morning takes some small comfort in knowing that the bird he is having little luck in finding is as ambiguous and indefinable as life itself. Evidence of the extent of the woodcock's whimsical nature lies in its colorful array of names: big-eyes, bogsucker, big mud snipe, Becasse, wood hen, mud bat, timber-doodle, and Labrador twister.

Scolopax minor. Swamp lover. The American wood-cock, an odd bird graced with even odder looks: great, dark, bulging eyes looking too big for the small head and set high on the narrow forehead; a long, thin bill; rounded wings attached to a short, stout body. Nothing seems to fit, make sense. The woodcock seems a gathering of stray avian parts, a misfit with wings. To the woodcock hunter all these oddities only deepen his obsession with this elusive, exasperating bird.

The woodcock is a difficult bird that delights in difficult places, such as murky sloughs and shadow-filled creek bottoms, any place clogged with thick undergrowth. Here the birds merge with the winter, are its colors on the wing: the subtle beauty of browns and blacks, flecks of grays and blemished whites, the color of leafless trees, spent fields, and dead grasses.

Woodcock nestle down amid thorns and briers and use their long bills to probe damp ground for earthworms, their favorite meal. The woodcock's bill is well-suited to the work of digging for worms. It's thought that nerves near the tip of the bill can sense whether worms have worked the soil recently. As long as a good piece of dense bottomland swamp has plenty of good cover and plenty of worms, there probably will be woodcock nearby. Only cold moves the birds. When the ground freezes, they leave, head south, often in great numbers. In years past large populations of migrating woodcock were common from the Southeast through the Gulf States. Continued drastic losses of wetland habitat, however, have resulted in dramatic losses of woodcock, especially along the Eastern Flyway, where during the last twenty years the woodcock population has declined more than 30 percent. The situation throughout the Central Flyway is, so far, less critical. Some wildlife biologists believe that 40 percent or more of the nation's migrating woodcock winter in the Louisiana area.

The woodcock has the distinction of being the only member of the sandpiper or shore bird family that is an upland game bird. Perhaps its genetic connection to shore birds accounts, in part, for the woodcock's bewildered looks, something suggesting a clumsy cross between a stilt sandpiper, a wandering tattler, and a grouse.

The day after weather reports called for a new push of cold, temperatures dropped 15 degrees. Moorfield got up at dawn; put on two shirts, a pair of heavy pants, three pairs of socks, and mud boots; had a quick cup of coffee; and walked down to the creek bottom. He took along his English setter named Dog and his old 28 gauge side-by-side shotgun; I carried my 20 gauge.

After daylight, when the sun is full and flat on the land, woodcock like to keep to the thick woods, tucked back among the cane and elder. Just at daylight and at dusk, when the light is soft and diffuse, they tend to move out into open fields to feed.

Moorfield walked along the creek bottom briskly, moving through knots of greenbrier as thorny as barbed wire as he whistled cheerfully. Signs of nearby birds were plentiful. By midmorning, Dog had flushed twelve birds, mostly females. Although there is little, if any, variation in the markings and coloring of woodcock, the females are larger, averaging about 8 ounces, while a big male rarely weighs more than 6 ounces.

The wind came up, stiff and cold, moving high among the trees, making a sound like old bones rattling. Dog knew the birds were at hand and eagerly worked the thick woods, ignoring the cold, living off the warmth of adrenaline and spent energy. Suddenly, a point, every muscle in the dog's body tense and certain. Clouds of his breath drifted up out of the woods like wisps of fog. No hesitation, no tentative suspicions, just pure bird. Dog knew, without a doubt.

Because so much of it takes place in dense cover, woodcock hunting is a drama that unfolds in a space of inches and feet rather than yards. Once a dog is onto a bird, once there is an honest point, all else depends on discipline and instinct, skill, tenacity, and a great helping of kind fortune.

Moorfield walked toward Dog, while never looking down at him, never looking at the ground. And then it was in the air, a knot of feathers whistling gently through the cold wind, a blur of golden browns, moody slate, grays, soft whites, as if someone had kicked up a pile of dead leaves and sent them spiraling in the wind. It didn't fly as much as it whirled, rising, dipping, twisting, then flinching right and left, more like a defective helicopter than a bird. Moorfield let loose with the 28 gauge as it climbed above the thick woods. A clear miss.

Unlike grouse or wild quail, a hunter's got to wait on woodcock to get even a possible shot. Woodcock hunting calls for real discipline—the patience to let the bird flush, get up, fly a few yards before taking a shot. It takes a long moment to decipher a woodcock's flight. In an instant, a flushed woodcock can ruin a bird hunter's health by, at once, spiraling, twisting, barrel-rolling, and corkscrewing through the air like a tiny, feathered dirigible with a serious leak.

The birds rose all morning, each flight a new education in the tenets of physics, the laws of motion and gravity. Einstein was right: everything is relative. It's all touch and go, especially on a winter morning in a deep Southern wood along a dark creek bottom, the cold pushing the men and woodcocks alike.

At day's end we had five nice birds, enough for a good, hot lunch—the birds spiced with garlic, a touch of red pepper and Tabasco sauce, and stuffed with pork sausage, and all of it over steaming rice.

"Hard not to love a bird this handsome and noble and crazy," Moorfield said as we walked back toward the house. He stopped, turned, looked at me with a sudden seriousness. "They are nuts, ya know. Really. I know a man over at the college, and he says the woodcock's brain is in upside down or something. Most of us have no excuse. The woodcock, though, he's naturally cracked-brained."

Moorfield, it turns out, is right, to a point. Compared to other birds, the woodcock's brain is at best an anomaly, for it indeed seems to be inverted, apparently upside down.

Woodcock. Timber-doodle. Mudbat. An erratic bird whose illogical twists and turns give a special beauty to winter's long, icy days, fill them with wonder, strange feats of aerial delight and that small sound of winter mornings and evenings—*pe-e-ent . . . pe-e-ent:* a tintinnabulation like a wind among ice-bound trees.

(1989)

Exultant Surprise

He would sit on the front porch for hours on fall days. Alice, his Gordon setter, sat near the steps, her nose to the wind. The dog's tail wagged incessantly, a barometer of the high emotion in the air.

They sat and listened to the birds in the near distance, across the pond, along a ragged thicket of wild plum and honeysuckle that edged a field of spent corn. In the nearly-palpable stillness of those autumn mornings, the male quails' whistles drifted on small winds, and the sound was as plaintive as a gospel verse. It was a sound that stirred something down deep in the old man and in me, an excitement that had lain dormant in us all year and now caught again, like a sudden spark in aged, dry wood.

As a young man, the old man had hunted them all. The weary woodcock, the roaring mountain grouse. But as a middle-aged bird hunter, he embraced monogamy. He cared for no game bird as he cared for quail. They had been on the land for as long as he could remember. In them he saw everything that was good about the land and the life he lived on it.

In those days, the land held an abundance of quail. There were fat years and lean years, to be sure, but come autumn, there was always the sound of wild coveys on the rise, the high-pitched whistle of frantic wings and a blur of feathers. All through the fall and winter and into the spring, whenever the weather held, we walked the fields and edges, the hedgerows and thickets, and every step was one of nearly-desperate expectation.

Quail hunting in the South has changed drastically since my grandfather's time. The agricultural economy of the South before World War II, a society of mostly small plantations and patch-quilt farms that allowed quail populations to thrive, is gone. Small farms have given way to enormous agricultural and lumbering enterprises. Consequently, vast tracts of prime quail habitat have been lost. As though swept aside by some plague, the great Southern quail populations have been decimated. Where quail once whistled in the still evenings by the thousands, there is now only silence.

There are still quail. Wild quail in large numbers still hang on in South Texas, Oklahoma, North Florida, and a few other regions. And throughout the South, there is a renewed determination to somehow save this endearing, tenacious Southern game bird, a bird that gave rise to an enduring legacy of outdoor life.

Research continues throughout the South and the nation. Most of it strives to understand quail, their complex lives, and their needs. Organizations like Quail Unlimited shoulder an unflagging belief that quail must always have a place in the South, in its future as well as its past. Toward this end, wildlife biologists at the Tall Timber Research Center in Florida and other such wildlife programs are working feverishly to solve the problem of whether man and quail can coexist.

Meanwhile, each fall and winter men are still drawn to the piney woods and open fields, to the thrill of watching lean, muscled bird dogs afield, to the sound of birds shattering still, heavy air. The time is coming, if indeed it has not already arrived, when Southern bird hunters must turn more and more to hunting reserves and preserves, to those places that have the knowledge, resources, and commitment to maintain and preserve traditional quail habitat. Unlike public hunting lands, private quail hunting reserves and plantations permit quail hunting season to open earlier and last longer, often until the end of March.

Of course, there is nothing new about private and commercial hunting clubs. Many date back at least fifty years or more. The more successful ones operating today—such as Westervelt Lodge in Alabama; Jimmy Bangs's Tallawahee Plantation near Dawson, Georgia; George HI Plantation in North Carolina; and Charlie Cannon's Pinefields in South Georgia—are run by men who have spent a lifetime on the land. They know it, understand it, and are devoted to it. They know what must be done, and their land shows the earmarks of sound wildlife management regular controlled burns to allow for good weed growth and proper sunlight penetration of woodlands. They leave old hedgerows and spent fields with edges that provide natural cover and food.

The Cannons have been on their South Georgia land for generations, and Charlie Cannon sees in Pinefields a way to share with others the lush heritage of Southern quail hunting on a sprawling piney wood plantation that has changed very little over the last half-century. When he decided to open Pinefields to bird hunting, Cannon wanted it to represent not only the polished and graceful traditions of Southern quail hunting but also the unequaled hospitality of the South.

For those who remember what Southern quail hunting was like, Pinefields is like coming home again. And for those who would like to sample the deep and lasting experience of Southern quail hunting, there is no finer or friendlier place to start. Pinefields is a tapestry of delicious food, gracious hospitality, and fellowship that soothes like a tonic. The lodge sits above a lake. Here, on the back porch each evening, exhausted hunters watch the diffused light of a dissolving winter sunset and swap tall tales, jokes, stories of hunts past and present, stories of legendary dogs, difficult shots, and unforgettable covey rises.

In the morning, come first light, it all begins. Four-wheel vehicles ferry hunters to the barn. From there transportation is a matter of choice. Some elect to ride the plantation wagon or join Charlie Cannon on horseback. A few want to take the Jeep with guide Ray Gene to try their luck at wild quail.

In looks, Ray Gene resembles Hank Williams, and he has more stories than Mark Twain. His face is a nomenclature of South Georgia's piney woods and its quail. Ray Gene stops at a field's edge, lets out two Brittanies and a pointer. He likes the little Brits. "They work tighter," he says. "They're loyal. A pointer ain't no good unless it's got at least three ribs showing." Ray Gene says this as if it were a scientific fact. "They gotta be rawboned and hungry because pointers ain't real loyal dogs. Brits, though. They're all heart and more agreeable than a wife." He tells George, the youngest Brittany, "to git with bird findin'." We follow George.

Spending a day afield with Ray Gene is worth the effort. In a patch of chest-high broomsedge, Ray Gene yelps at George, "Stay close in here." George needs little encouragement. He and the others quarter the field, heads working the wind. "George'll smile if he locks onto a covey," says Ray Gene. "I mean a toothy grin. He's a natural showoff."

All of a sudden, Ray Gene spots a Cooper's hawk flying low over the next pea field. Birds. What the hawk tells Ray Gene, the wind has already told the dogs. They are all three frozen near a clump of tangled sumac along an old hedgerow. "Trust 'em," says Ray Gene. "These dogs know things we ain't never gonna know." Like a Roman candle, the covey explodes from the thicket, flying low over the field and veering off toward every point of the compass. Shotguns report. Two birds go down. Wild Southern bobwhite quail. Worth the day, the aching muscles, the scratched arms and hands, the soaking feet. The pointer retrieves, and George is sitting in the dirt road, his fur full of briers, smiling his toothy grin.

That night, there is talk that Southern quail have not gone. They are just wilder, warier, harder to find. We all want to believe that. I always want there to be quail, quail to rise with exultant surprise from some old matted hedgerow and set my heart to racing and lead me across an empty winter field to I know not where.

(1988)

Gobblers in the Mist

November moon, low in the sky, and full. The rolling Alabama hill country looks like a badly underexposed photograph: stark whites and deep blacks. E.D. Earl's grocery, an old church, farm houses with rusting tin roofs, the weathered tombstones of small, crumbling cemeteries are all soaked in moon glow and shine like soapstone. It is 3 AM on the back roads of Chambers and Randolph counties.

The woods here are wide and dense, mixed hardwoods and shortneedle pine, mostly, and everywhere sprawling knots of muscadine, blueberry, trumpet, and shuffledine vines, dog fennel, and sumac. Turkey country: some of the best in the South, some of the best in the nation, and some of the best in Alabama, a state heralded for its beautiful turkey woods. The turkeys are here, near at hand. You can sense them in the darkness like a slight press of wind against the skin.

I kill the truck's motor near the ridge above the creek bottom. I am on the west side of the Tallapoosa River at the north end of the 2,600 acres in Randolph County leased by Rockfence Station, one of Alabama's finest hunting clubs.

Hours earlier, at dusk, I was here in these same thick woods, down along the creek, well hidden, waiting and watching, knowing they would come.

It was late; the light was fading, flat and opaque. The turkeys would be roosting soon. Surely, they would come this way.

I heard them behind me, a soft rustle among the leaves and scrub. There were thirteen in all, eight gobblers and five hens.

They moved easily along the far side of the creek, feeding in the dissolving light, moving up the bank toward the oaks and pines. The day's last light burned down to a dull gold, and suddenly they took wing, flying up into the trees. Their wings produced a sound like kettle drums being played in an empty concert hall.

When the evening star gained the ridgeline, I eased from my warren quietly, moved down the creek bottom, then up to the ridge along an old logging road. Night drifted down like fog, settling first in the hollows and along the creek bottom and at the river's edge. The wind came up hard and cold as I got to the truck farther up on the abandoned, rutted road.

Fall turkey hunting is far less popular than the traditional spring hunting season, and with good reason. It lacks the great high drama of the spring hunt. Come spring, gobblers take on the life of truculent loners, edgy bachelors eager to assemble their harem of hens. All else irritates and upsets them.

Like any man with woman troubles, they are gloomy, nervous, morose, petulant, suspicious of everything in their world, even each other. It takes all of a hunter's skill and luck to first find a big gobbler and then call him up, seduce him with fraudulent, raspy notes of love so tempting he cannot resist.

It is man and turkey at first light, one on one. Even so, it is never really a fair contest. The wild turkey holds all the aces, which is only as it should be. After all, it is the turkey's life, not the hunter's, that is on the line.

Fall wild turkey hunting is much different, less frustrating, less strained and perplexing. Indeed, turkey hunters who consider themselves purists believe fall turkey hunting is something of a mockery of all they love and treasure about the sport. It isn't a fair fight, they say, and there is some truth to their argument.

In the fall and winter, wild turkeys tend to flock up, move about in droves, some of which can be quite large. Pressed by the unrelenting cold, gobblers seem less wary, less aggressive, burdened by fewer suspicions. Banding together, the birds seem less concerned for their safety than their survival.

Nonetheless, there is, for me, a unique beauty and challenge and purpose to fall turkey hunting. When I was a boy, I lived for a time on my grandfather's place in the Ozark Mountains of Arkansas. Every fall, close to Thanksgiving, we would go into the hills and take one turkey: food for the Thanksgiving table. The season, the hunt, the bird—all were part of our personal fete, a celebration not only of our good fortune to be on the land, but of the land itself.

In the fall, the quiet is as wide as it is deep; in the spring, dawn brings a grating cacophony of curious howls, squeaks, clucks, yips, warbles, cackles, yelps, peeps, and nasal gobbles. Not from turkeys, but rather from turkey hunters armed with the latest bizarre array of gadgets and gimmicks, each one guaranteed to lure wild turkeys closer.

But on this fall morning in Randolph County, when even the rising sun will bring no warmth, I keep it simple. No camouflage; just old work clothes, dull greens and browns, an old battered gray hat, and a heavy blue jacket.

The old turkey wing bone call is in my left shirt pocket. Once white, the smooth bone has gone yellow with the years. The wing bone is simple, reliable. The charm of the wing bone is that, like wild turkeys, it rarely produces the same sound twice. Wild turkeys distrust the predictable, especially when it comes to sound.

It doesn't take much to get a turkey's attention: one alluring note on the wing bone can be as tempting as a whole symphony played to perfection on a fancy mouth call. It's not the call or the caller that's important, finally, but the honesty of the sound produced. And the wing bone always gives me a good yelp, original and different every time.

The rutted logging road bends down along the creek bottom, down where the night is as dark as a raven's wing. Off the road, tangles of vines grab at my feet and legs.

Every brittle leaf crushed underfoot, every snapped twig is a heartbreak, the turkey's ally, a signal of my presence as loud and as clear as a siren blast. My movements become slower and more precise than a mime's as I work my way to within 50 feet of the roost trees.

Done fairly, fall turkey hunting means getting the birds off their roost trees, then creeping in behind them, hiding, and trying to call them back. I like stacking the contest further in the turkey's favor by moving away from the roost trees and trying to lure a gobbler in my direction. This way success depends as much on chance as skill, which is as it should be. Getting a wild turkey in the fall takes little effort, unless the effort is added.

At dawn, I rise from behind a fallen log yowling, kicking up leaves, flapping my arms. The birds come off the trees in bursts of sudden sound, their drumming wings sending small peals of thunder over the creek bottom. Even before they hit the ground, I move from my hiding place, hurry up the creek bottom, past the roost trees, then slightly north to the big oak I had noticed at sunset.

I feel the bite of the oak's rough bark along my spine, hunker down in its shadow, rub the old wing bone as though it were Mother Luck, and put it to my lips. A yelp, nothing panicky, yet still urgent. One, then another, then silence. Patience, patience as the oak's shadow thins in the daylight. Another yelp, louder, bolder.

And they are there in the near distance, below the roost trees, about 60 yards downhill. Three of them, one hen and two gobblers. By now the oak's bark feels like rough-edged bolts digging into my back, but I don't move. Instead, I concentrate on slowing my breathing. The shotgun is at my shoulder, safety off, feeling heavy as an anvil. The muscles in my shoulders tremble. Another minute, long. The lead turkey moves off to the left. It is the older of the two, sporting a 10- or 11-inch beard and fine, knotty spurs. A noble bird, one for the spring, when the whole thing will be on his terms. Behind him a smaller male, still a nice bird, sure to go more than 15 pounds.

Another yelp, and the two gobblers move up the creek bottom to my right. A fog has settled along the creek, and the birds seem to float above the earth like specters. The seconds bring them closer, closer, moving as quietly as a breeze: 30 yards, 20 yards. In the building light I can see the glint of the dawn in their eyes. The smaller gobbler moves nervously near my hiding place.

My finger wraps around the trigger as I breathe in deeply and slowly, carefully sighting down the barrel at the darting head of the young gobbler. I squeeze the trigger, and as the young turkey drops, I catch a glimpse of the lead bird, the big gobbler vanishing well back into the fog, safe in its wild blood. Until spring.

(1989)

How Do You Account
for the Luck Some Folks
Have with Rod and Gun?

Last Easter my neighbor George Turlow (as I shall call him) and his family sat down to eat a holiday turkey. It was no supermarket bird, but one shot by Turlow a few weeks earlier on a chilly March morning in Louisiana—just fifteen minutes after he got out of his Jeep and crossed the river into the woods, with his Browning shotgun and a pocket full of shells. The turkey, a fair-sized tom, was nonchalantly feeding in the tall bulrushes by the river's edge. It was almost as though the turkey was waiting to be found by Turlow. I was behind him fumbling for a Kleenex when he got his bird. It seems I'm always just a step behind Turlow. His day's hunt completed while the morning fog still lay thick in the woods' low places, Turlow carried his bird back to the Jeep, drank hot coffee, balanced his checkbook and dozed. I returned at noon, my lips chapped from five hours of turkey calling. It wasn't a good morning. I had only got the attention of five hunting dogs, a curious raccoon, a coyote, a wild rooster, and a snickering game warden. Turlow shrugged his shoulders and smiled. He's always shrugging his shoulders and smiling.

Last deer season there was but one buck taken by a member of the Full Moon Hunting Club. It was Turlow's deer, all six points of it. On that cold December morning Turlow had just sat down to his usual camp breakfast of hot grits and orange juice when the deer showed up outside the door of the shack. Turlow, dressed in underwear and black cowboy boots, dispatched the deer and was back at his breakfast before his grits had cooled. I went into the woods thirty-nine days last year, leaving most mornings before dawn and without benefit of breakfast, subsisting instead on a Spartan diet of cold coffee and cheese crackers, and came out of the woods at winter's end with blisters, leg cramps, and a nagging cough that for weeks threatened to turn into pneumonia.

When we went up into the mountains looking to fill our creels with trout, Turlow contentedly fished a small section of a mountain stream that supposedly had been fished out years ago. By noon Turlow had a 2-pound trout frying in his black skillet and was resting comfortably beneath a willow tree, thumbing through several outdoor catalogs. I was down to my last fly and hadn't even latched on to a good-size tree limb all morning. Moody and sunburned, I drove into town for a McDonald's fish sandwich.

Turlow makes his own duck calls out of thin pieces of mahogany, rubber bands, and glue. He keeps three on hand at all times, never knowing when a skein might fly overhead, and the ducks respond to his calls with almost gleeful enthusiasm, all but jumping into his game bag. There seems to be no fowl with which he cannot strike up a conversation. I hunted ducks with Turlow one day last year. He took his limit of birds in twenty minutes.

I like Turlow, but honestly, I have my suspicions about the guy. After all, it's hard to completely trust a man who, in twenty-eight years as an outdoorsman, has never so much as had his cap knocked off by a stray branch, tripped headfirst into a slough with his brand-new shotgun, lost his best hunting dog (the one with the inbred, infallible homing instinct), or lied to his friends about the size of his first deer or his last fish. Turlow never misplaces his rod and reel, puts his hunting license through the wash, or spills maple syrup over the stock of his deer rifle. His fishing tackle never snaps; his shotgun never jams; his waders never tear or leak. Turlow's wife has never used his best monofilament line to tie up the tomatoes and peas. Indeed, Turlow's wife tolerates his love of sport and the outdoors and willingly spends her weekends washing and polishing his Jeep, Scotchgarding his clothes, steam-drying his flies, and renewing his subscriptions to outdoor magazines. While his children mend his tent, mine use ours for a playhouse; it now has finger-painted walls and extra doors.

There is something just plain unnatural about Turlow. Nobody is supposed to have it that good. Most men live lives that are at best tossed salads, a mixture of good times and bad. An ordinary man might spend any number of cold winter mornings sitting stiff-backed 20 feet up in a beech tree munching cheese crackers just in the hope of seeing a big buck take shape out of the fog at the river's edge. Turlow never gets stiff; his luck goes on and on. What's worse, none of it seems to rub off, no matter how close you stay to him. I have followed him into the same beanfield, armed with the identical shotgun and shells, dressed in the same brand of pants, shirt, and boots, chewing the same brand of bubble gum, wearing a baseball cap with the same logo on it, smelling of the same after-shave lotion, and have matched him shot for shot. And at day's end I have helped Turlow carry his limit of birds out of the same field, the better able to do so because I have bagged none.

Turlow is pretty closemouthed about his luck; he says only that he's always been sort of lucky, always seems to be in the right place at the right time, and that he thinks "it all has something to do with being born under a full hunter's moon." Some members of the Full Moon Hunting Club are out to get Turlow, to turn his luck sour. There's talk of letting the air out of his Jeep tires, of punching holes in his mosquito netting, of diluting his bug dope with sugar water. Instead, I've decided to stick close to Turlow, never let him out of my sight, no matter how many trout streams, beanfields, and forests I have to follow him into.

(1982)

A Hunting Dog's
Days Afield

Thurber was my grand-father's dog, a handsome Gordon setter that was all muscle and excitement and determination. I have never known another living thing that loved adventure and the scent of trouble on the wind as much as Thurber. Although he was somewhat short on pedigree and prestige, he had real heart and an indomitable character. While he was alive, Thurber ran the old man's place and everything and everyone on it, including me and my grandfather. The truth to tell, neither one of us would have had it any other way.

He was a complex dog, given to sudden fits and starts. As a young puppy, with auburn hair and shining eyes, he insisted on joining my grandfather in a short drink of bourbon one evening. It had been my grandfather's habit for sixty years. It instantly became Thurber's habit as well and perhaps accounts for some of his good-natured eccentricities.

Thurber was a confusing and mildly perplexing name for a hunting dog, especially one from Arkansas. To everyone in the county's utter bewilderment, my grandfather named him that in honor of the humorist and cartoonist James Thurber. The dogs that tiptoed and blundered through Thurber's delightful cartoons always seemed slightly bewildered, a condition our own Thurber suffered from, especially on cold and wet November days when he would go bursting into the thick cover of Mallard Slough, his nose full of moving woodcock. He would exit soaked and smiling, his hide a pincushion of briers and thorns. He rarely found the birds, but how he loved the heady adventure.

The old man never really considered Thurber as just a dog. He was family, friend, companion, confidant. Thurber lacked the nobility, class, and manners of an English setter and the gritty, rawboned, almost machine-like, emotionless dependability of a sleek, tireless pointer. But he loved the dark, deep woods as much as any other dog, and nothing in life escaped either his unquenchable curiosity or stubborn attention. Thurber was not a seasonal dog. He didn't work the bird season then stretch out on the porch for the remainder of the year doting on his good luck, good fortune, and good bloodline. To Thurber, there were no such things as seasons, opening days, and closing days.

When my grandfather and I put up the shotguns and took out the fly rods, Thurber was near at hand. He met us at the back door as he always did, that unmistakable crooked smile on his face and his eyes bright with anticipation. Fishing, at least to the irrepressible Thurber, was for years nothing more than an elaborate game of throw and fetch. And Thurber dearly loved to fetch, especially trout flies. When I finally saved up enough money to invest in my first really good fly rod, an 8.5-foot R.L. Winston imported from Twin Bridges, Montana, it was Thurber who took the package carefully from the post office and carried it 2 miles from town with a certain pride and grace, as if he knew what the long package contained.

By the way, Thurber finally did catch on to trout fishing. He got so he would lie on his belly beside the stream in the tall grass, usually beside a large, still pool of water. He would keep this vigil sometimes for hours. Thurber had the patient heart of a true fly-fisherman. He knew there was a brook trout in that pool, and he was just waiting. When he saw the fish's dark shadow in the clear water, he quivered and shook all over, so great was his excitement. Never taking his eyes off the rising trout, he would pounce without hesitation, hitting the water quickly and with the sudden impact of a dislodged boulder. For the most part, the trout escaped, shaken and nervous, but alive.

For a hunting dog, a dog harassed by constant thoughts and dreams of rising birds, Thurber had a good disposition. While he was skeptical of most strangers, he rarely bit anyone, and if he did, he bit them only once—on the theory that the experience had probably taught them a useful lesson. This was one of Thurber's obscure but somehow delightful rituals that those who knew him and loved him accepted and never really tried to completely figure out. Several ladies in town blamed Thurber's unexplained temper on his lack of breeding. After all, they pointed out, he had come from Maryland. No one in the county had ever been to Maryland, although some of the old-timers remembered that during the War of Northern Aggression (also known as the Civil War), Maryland had been a fence sitter, unable to put a firm grasp on its loyalties.

Actually, as his papers showed, he was born in a kennel of good reputation near the things he loved best—water, woods, and wildlife of every description just waiting to be sniffed out, discovered. Gordon setters, once popular bird dogs, had by that time fallen out of favor with bird hunters and been replaced by English setters and pointers. The kennel owner was stuck with ten Gordon setter puppies. He ran an ad in an outdoor magazine asking $20 a puppy, no questions asked, no refunds, and no returns. Two weeks later, Thurber, packed in a large crate with plenty of holes and lots of straw, landed at the Little Rock airport. Set loose, he licked my grandfather and growled meekly at the luggage handler. Thurber was always a dog of strict loyalties.

He grew into a fine dog, almost regal in bearing, powerful and yet gentle and graceful. His tail never stopped, not even when pointing birds. From the beginning, life for Thurber was perpetual excitement. If his life lacked a certain profound philosophy, it was overflowing with purpose. As far as I know, he had only two fears—one was of being mistakingly left behind. Because of this, he was always the first one up, tapping his tail on the wooden floor while the rest of us searched for clothes, reached for coffee and bacon, hunted for misplaced shotguns. Ever anxious, Thurber would run to the back door and wait there, nervously watching the sun rise. Storms also upset him, left him queasy. While he enjoyed a good duck hunt in an icy rain, not even a flock of mallards or grouse could coax him out of the house during a thunderstorm. Thunder left him visibly shaken, as though each loud, pounding noise rolling down the valley were a personal portent of doom. Thurber embellished these atmospheric histrionics by quickly bolting under the closest bed, where he stayed until the "all clear" was sounded. Thurber had a well-honed sense of catastrophe and worried why others didn't see the gravity of these meteorological upheavals and follow his warnings and leap for safety.

———⟩•◇•⟨———

It was December when I found him, a week before Christmas, his favorite holiday. (He delighted in dragging in the Christmas tree, thinking there might be birds hidden in it. He watched over it for days for any sign of avian life.) I found his body near the headwaters of Big Creek not far from where the drove of old turkeys roosted. I carried him back to the house, following an old trail he had worn through the oak hummock. The day was cold, with a freezing wind blowing out of Oklahoma. My grandfather stood at the back door. I could see the sadness etched on his face. He went to the barn for a shovel, and we buried Thurber out past the garden near a thicket of honeysuckle where the quail sometimes gathered. Grandfather placed a simple red brick where we laid him.

Even today, I remember him by the fire, a grand dog lost in dream, his hind legs kicking. While dreaming, no bird in the county ever escaped him. He was devoted to life and had spent his years tirelessly exploring, excavating, botanizing, observing, hunting, fetching, finding. As my grandfather said years later, Thurber was a dog who knew and appreciated the value and importance of life. And every morning he rushed down the stairs and out the back door of the old house to greet it and warm himself in its glow.

(1987)

JOURNEYING

The Fisherman's Dream

$\mathbf{T}$o separate it from my other mental wanderings, which are considerable, I call this dream a dozing musing.

When the dream comes, it is nearly always the same, an ethereal journey to some distant, yet familiar, Southern mountain river or stream. Spooky, shadowy trout, some as big and long as creel bags, fill these racing waters like visions radiant in color and light and motion. The dream is a comfort, settling in my imagination where it builds fantastic castles in the air out of drowsiness and cadenced breathing.

My dream always comes bearing gifts—travel, willowy cane rods and tough, reliable reels, peace and contentment on cold winter days, sweet delusions of fat trout rising to my dry fly—presented perfectly, of course, without flaw or error. The older I become, the more this lovely dream of trout and Southern streams soothes me. My closest friends, those lithe 9-foot graphite companions, are with me, never fail me. Sometimes their names, like the sound of a mountain creek, are like a mantra—Powell, Nicholas Whipp, Sage, R. L. Winston.

While I muse about trout, Cody, my Labrador retriever, is busy waging a personal vendetta against a number of our neighbors, including a gray squirrel, a family of raccoons, a bashful skunk, my son's soccer ball, and several pieces of lawn furniture. Cody is a dog of purpose and conviction, and it is his firm conviction that the world would be a safer and saner place without such things.

In my unfolding chimera, it is early spring, and I have packed the car with all I need and all the extras. Included are reels from the House of Hardy and Scientific Angler; plenty of line; weights 4 and 5; small boxes bulging with armies of dry flies—all little well-groomed bundles of fur and feathers in a delightful rainbow of colors; and my old, well-worn, heavy green waders, which have been patched so many times that they look to suffer from a rare but unhealthy fungus, a plague of brown patches spreading from toe to waist. Then I am off, bound for a journey of consequence, as every angling journey surely is.

While there is a consoling unity to my nightly dream of fish, I never fish the same stream twice. While on some icy January night, I am working a No. 12 Elk Wing caddis over Karen's Pool on Holcomb Creek; two nights later, I'm fishing my loyal Royal Coachman on the gin-clear waters of Collins Creek in the Smoky Mountains. Come February, I am standing in a big dory drifting in one of the Hiwassee River's big pools, flicking the bright-yellow weighted line and a 12.5-foot leader, 4x tippet, and No. 14 white Royal Wulff over a sleek rainbow trout.

By month's end, I am up on the Rapidan in the Blue Ridge Mountains of Virginia dressed in shorts, a T-shirt, and hip boots. Perfection escapes me even in fantasy, and this somehow disappoints me, though I am pleased that I seem to handle needle knots, perfection knots, and surgeon knots better unconscious than conscious. I like fishing the Rapidan, especially that part of it that flows swiftly over smooth stones through the Shenandoah National Park. Barbless hooks only. All trout must be released. Insurance for the future. I wouldn't have it any other way. Each trout is more than a mere fish; it is a thrill, a living memory and experience that can be relived again and again.

On the Little River in the Smokies, I become a trout tracker, a sneak thief, crawling hunchbacked over giant gray stones that stand at the edge of quiet pools of clear waters. On my stomach looking down, I can see the big brown trout just below the surface, his nose pointed upstream. Magnified by the water, he looks enormous. I kneel on the stone as still as a reptile in the sun, slowly dapping my shortened line and fly, a tempting, wriggling hopper, above his nose. Colored shards of light drift on the gleaming pool, and then it explodes into a violence of thrashing water as the big trout leaps to devour my small, fraudulent offering. Gently, I ease the small hook from his lip, release him back into the shining pool where he is noble and above all things.

And I go on, from pool to pool.

Mostly, my luck doesn't hold. The trout spook at the smallest shadow. They are the wariest of fish even in my untroubled dream. When it comes to trout, a dreaming angler is asking for as much trouble as a fully conscious one. Trout fishermen are always candidates for piscatorial torment.

But my winter dream does succeed in removing some obstacles, irritations. The rivers are never dry or without fish; I slip less often, my line never knots or tangles; I always select the right fly and always catch fish; and I usually rest at noon on some rock as big as a Cadillac, where there is a thin mist rising off the river and the air smells of wild ginger. At the river's edge, there is a garland of wildflowers.

And then, I am in the river again, switching from a Quill Gordon to a March Brown, which I groom and fluff as though I were sending it off to its first day of school. I cast. Nothing great. The Whipp rod makes me more of a fly-fisherman than I am. At least there is no drag. A pleasing compromise between the real and the unreal. I am casting smoothly, with deliberate rhythm, the looping line and supple rod momentarily joining me with the unending cycle of fish and river and insect and mountain solitude. One of the great charms of Southern trout fishing is that so many of the better trout streams are sometimes difficult to get to. To a fly-fisherman, a crowd is one angler and two fish.

In my angling dream, there is always ample time for rest, a time for shedding the heavy, hot waders, carefully setting the rods against a huge hemlock tree, sitting on the bank eating Vienna sausage and crackers and drinking ice water from the canteen. A kingfisher squawks downriver. I whistle back. Just two anglers exchanging streamside gossip. And I rest on the bank: a dream inside a dream, a thought that this is what I really fish for, a deep feeling of satisfaction and stormless serenity. As the alarm sounds and my wife stirs, and Cody yawns, the last thing I recall is a dimple on the river's surface and the speckled shadow of a rising trout.

(1988)

Spring on the Miramichi

Studying a map of New Brunswick only reinforces the actual experience of driving through this great hunk of sprawling Canadian landscape, giving extra detail to the sense of its vastness and, in places, its remoteness, the wild edge that marks it from mountains to ragged Atlantic coast. Isolated, somehow disconnected for a moment from the great sprawl of Canada, New Brunswick resembles a great tattered isle populated only at the fringes, with the great woods, a scattering of nervous small towns and villages. To the north is Campbellton at the narrow neck of the Baie des Chaleurs. Down the Atlantic coast Shediac, Sackville off the Cumberland Basin, St. John on the teeming waters of Edmundston. The largest city any distance inland is Fredericton, capital of the province.

In the early spring, New Brunswick's weather is a chaos, not of patterns, but of assaults. It is weather with teeth and a sense of irony. On the same day it can be mild and balmy as a tropical island at St. George and snowing hard out of a yowling wind up in Northumberland district, along Nepisiquit River near Mount Carleton.

On the afternoon I left Fredericton for the Miramichi River country, a day when I should have had nothing on my mind but leaping Atlantic salmon (*Salmo salar*) and the great river, wide with the ice melt and early rains, and surely thick with salmon, I was instead confronted by fog, a fog so vile it looked as though it had just rolled off the dark walls of the north Atlantic. It was like driving through an endless pall, some wet, viscid shroud covering the entire countryside. Finally, the road itself seemed to fall away, disappear, and I was left driving on faith, heading generally toward the town of Doakville at a hesitant 15 miles an hour, as Fredericton was enveloped in an immense glacier of fog. Fredericton is known for its stately elms, its lush greens, the skilled artisans of the New Brunswick Craft School, and the cherub atop the fountain at city hall known affectionately as "Freddie, the Little Nude Dude." It is also known among Canadians as the poet's city, being the home of Sir Charles G.D. Roberts, Jonathon Odell, Bliss Carman, and Francis Joseph Sherman.

Ahead, Highway 8 stretches like a black ribbon in the gray fog, edging into the great Miramichi Basin, a vast tapestry of streams and rivers and lakes radiating out from the Miramichi River. The thick woods are full of spruce and fir. There is the heavy smell of hemlock and juniper on the wind. It is a countryside of great beauty and an allure as strong and natural as the pull of gravity. This is country for hiker, canoeist, bird hunter, and especially the salmon angler.

The river's name is from the Micmac Indians who thought of the river as sacred, the haunt of spirits, a place of great power. Those who call the river valley home continue to believe in the Miramichi's special character. To come from the land of the Miramichi is to be greatly blessed, an argument that is hard to contest, once you have given into the river and the land through which it inexorably moves.

Ernest Long was born on the river and its mark is on him, in his infectious smile and laugh, in his manner and character. As a Canadian paratrooper for nineteen years, Long has seen the world and much of its beauty and mystery, but still no piece of the earth affects him like the Miramichi. To it he has always returned. Long will proudly tell you that even while in the service, he only missed one salmon season on the river. The river is in him and he is in it. It is a trait common along this great salmon river. Those fortunate to call this land home rarely leave it, or if they do, as Long did, they nearly always return, driven perhaps by the same undeniable instinct for home that drives the river's Atlantic salmon on their long and often brutal migration each year back, not to just any salmon river, but only this river, the river of their youth, the river they recognize and separate from all others by its smell, the feel of it through their gills.

On our first day on the river together, Long stopped the boat for a moment near Duff Pond to show me the bright white frame house up on the high bank, above the flood-line, where he was born. He took his first bright salmon on the river before he reached the age of twelve and started guiding the anglers at Wilson's Sport Fishing Camps when he was fourteen. Keith Wilson pulls his boat beside us. Keith is the fourth generation of Wilson to run the camp. He tells me that it has been a good year, all things considered for the salmon; they are here. The angling has been good, especially just before I arrived. Naturally.

There are four anglers in camp. A good number. The Miramichi can swallow up four salmon anglers in a hurry, make you feel as though the whole river and every salmon in it have been reserved for you. Keith shows us to our cabins across the street from the old Wilson home-place that now serves as the dining room and lodge. The Wilsons have been guiding anglers on the Miramichi since 1929, making their camp the longest running family-owned fishing camp on the river. The cabins are simple, comfortable. Everything but telephones and televisions, which, of course, are among the things salmon anglers are trying to escape from, however briefly. Salmon flash in the big pond in front of the old house and the Canadian flag snaps in a cold, early spring wind. As we cross the street, Keith motions to the pond. "There's a seven-pound brook trout in there I can't catch," he says with a shrug of his shoulders. There is a noticeable quickening of our paces as we near the cabin and our flyrods.

Before dinner that first evening, there is a ritual pilgrimage from the lodge on Newman Road in McNamee, five miles north of Boiestown, into Doaktown, where there is a museum celebrating the river country and the Atlantic salmon, considered here and elsewhere to be the king of sportfish, the royal head of the Salmo or trout family. Nearby is yet another angling institution, Doak's Fly and Tackle Shop, where two generations of the Doak family have tended to the needs of fishermen, whether locally made salmon flies, level-headed advice, or as level-headed as a man can be about Atlantic salmon, or a place where the vexed and the lucky can spin their salmon tales. I leave with a pocketful of colorful smelt flies and Golden Eagles. "They're a sure thing," says one of the shop's local customers. "Took me two salmon on one this mornin a'ya." I also grabbed a handful of Elmer's Specials, just in case, and Jerry Doak smiled and said, "Best to take a selection. Locals been known to tell a tale or two about what flies are good just to keep other anglers off the fish." The atmosphere of the shop seems composed almost entirely of spent anglers' breath, as the little crowd of fishermen reassure each other that salmon are complex and difficult fish, impossible to figure out, which only increases its nobility and mystery, qualities that trout anglers find particularly irresistible. The more upsetting a fish, the greater its allure. And Atlantic salmon are forever unpredictable, a source of constant surprise. Like the river itself and press of the new season, they are different, not only from day to day, but from moment to moment, at once exasperating and exhilarating.

We are up at first light, bundled in layers of warm clothes, ready to fish. Breakfast first. It's tradition, after all. The salmon have waited this long; we convince ourselves another hour won't completely put them off. The lodge is soaked in the smell of fresh hot sausage, bacon, homemade biscuits and pancakes, eggs cooked to every taste, homemade jellies and preserves, hot coffee and tea, hot cereals. On and on. While we eat, Keith reads from the camp's log, letting us know how the last batch of anglers did. Keith's voice rises like steam. The room is warm, the food is warm, everything seems to glow in warm comfort. Keith's voice rises like steam from a kettle. Meanwhile, outside it is raining ice.

Two to a boat: one angler and a guide. I ride with Ernest Long. In the rain, his ruddy, wind-burned face is as red as an overripe tomato. He is chewing on the stub of a cigar. Long, an inveterate storyteller, laughs easily and often, punctuating his every pause with the ubiquitous end mark "a'ya," which seems to be the Canadian equivalent of the American "ya know." Long has been on the river all his life; there is plenty to tell, plenty he's seen.

"Sports are always entertaining folks, a'ya. Anglers like to gossip about guides and it's only natural that guides like to gossip about all the sports they've taken out. Some are just plain curious, a'ya." Knowing that you are bound to become one of Long's tales makes an angler check his idiosyncrasies, keep them in hand or out of sight.

The wind rubs against the skin as though it had nails. The skin chaps quickly, especially the lips, then cracks. The ice stops, the day is cold and sunless and gray, and I let out my line as Long anchors the boat bow to the current. We are, at once, thoroughly miserable and completely happy. The reason for both conditions is the same: salmon.

Since commercial netting of salmon is no longer allowed on the river, the salmon have begun to come back, increasing every year, allowing the Miramichi to reclaim its place as one of the few truly premier salmon rivers left in North America. Wilson's Sport Fishing Camp has five miles of water on the river, including more than fifteen of the best salmon pools on the river, pools with names like Coldwater, Home Pool, Big Murphy, Buttermilk, and Little Murphy Pool. In the summer, once the river drops, anglers are taken to pools by canoe. For spring fishing, though, since the river is high from ice melt, snow, and rain, john boats fitted with small motors are used. Near Little Murphy Pool, our second stop of the morning, I let the current take 25 feet of line, then pulled slightly against the drag, a small flinch once and I could feel the strike. The fish is a grilse, a salmon that has been to sea only a year, a fish not fully matured, at least in the angler's eye, a sort of novice adventurer, a salmon in adolescent's clothing. It put up a strong fight, though, running up and across stream before finally tiring, giving in. Long brought it in carefully with the net, gently let it go. Long lights a fresh cigar. This is something he does to mark the first fish of the day. "I tell you Wilson's had the best stretch of water on the whole river. I've fished it all, the whole thing from Half Moon down, and if you can't get a fish at Home Pool, then you can't get a fish."

Shore lunch is at Murphy's Camp. The fire feels good. So does the coffee, the hot tea, the fresh salmon steak, and the simmering Canadian hash. Everyone has at least one new salmon story to tell in between gulps of coffee, bites of salmon, and time as close to the fire as possible. As with breakfast, there is too much of everything. There is more to Wilson's than the fishing; there is the food, which is bountiful and generous and seems to never stop coming. Four hours after lunch we are back at the lodge sitting down to an abundant meal of soups and salads, salmon and hollandaise sauce, hot, freshly baked bread, three different vegetables, mashed potatoes, coffee, tea, and three different homemade cakes and pies. Recovery from such a meal takes time, and Keith Wilson makes the time pass more pleasantly by telling us the story of one Stanley Church of New Jersey who, in 1964, took during his stay at the camp 259 grilse and salmon. Afterwards, Keith takes up his log and goes around asking each of us what luck we had on the day. Having heard of Mr. Church's luck, our voices are low and modest. As for me, I whispered, two grilse, one brook trout, one salmon.

But as the days went on, the weather and our luck and the angling improved. We fished and talked of the salmon, of its complex and complicated life, its struggle for survival against acid rain, pollution, dams, and especially commercial fishing. Big, silver salmon took our flies hungrily and fought with an unyielding ferocity, going deep, twisting, turning, finally leaping, their heavy, muscled flanks flashing like mirrors in the soft, spring sunshine. We let them go easily, gently, watching them go deep, disappear in the dark water, the wildness full and uncompromised.

Each salmon that struck was not just a salmon, but a Miramichi Salmon, marked by the river, destined to return here and only here, rather than perhaps the great salmon rivers of Iceland, the United Kingdom, Norway, or any other Canadian salmon river. Only here, to the Miramichi. Here they began as alevins, and some survived to become parr, fish that would stay in the river for up to two years before they would, should they survive, undergo yet another transformation and develop into smolts, fish up to two feet long, fish ready to follow their salmon blood, move into the cold Atlantic for the great salmon migration to the feeding grounds off the coast of Greenland. Those who survived would be back. Some would come in a couple of years; others later, but they would come back. "Sort of like me," says Ernest Long. "I left as a young man, went off saw the world, but I had to come back. I ended up where I began, the Miramichi, home. Perhaps that's why I like them so. We've traveled the same road, I think, and come to the same conclusion. There's no place like this river. No place at all."

(1991)

The Green Canoe

The season does not matter. Along this river, in these woods, mornings have a symmetry about them. I wake at dawn. Last night's fire is still warm. With but a little kindling, it takes hold quickly, chasing off the morning's chill. Breakfast is simple: bacon, biscuits, orange juice. Later, everything packed, I clear the campsite, even burying the fire's ashes, covering my presence with leaves and fallen limbs.

Knee-deep in the river's cool water, I load the green canoe. In the faint, wispy morning sunlight, the river takes on the delicate color of a blue-green gem. The water holds the sunlight like a prism. Colors flash everywhere on the river's surface. I ease the canoe over bits of stone and dirt and into the river, the upper James in the mountains of Virginia. Pulling my rumpled, old, brown Clancy hat low over my eyes, I direct the green canoe into the river's pressing current with a few firm, deep strokes of the smooth ash-wood paddle. We move steadily downriver, the green canoe and I, the sun warm, rising, hauling the new day with it. There is no better way, I think, to get to know and appreciate so many of the South's splendid and beautiful rivers than by floating them in a good, sturdy canoe.

My canoe, this green canoe, is small, meant only for a party of one. Mostly, I do my river traveling alone. The green canoe is a used canoe. I do not, however, mind used gear. This old canoe has probably seen more rivers than I will ever know. Somehow knowing this reassures me. It is good to have such an experienced partner under me, its battered nose pointed confidently downstream. Looking at the equipment stowed in the canoe now, I am not surprised to learn that most of it is secondhand, even my hat, which I got off a fly fisherman I met on the Bullpasture River in Virginia.

He was a visitor from New Zealand, and he was catching plenty of trout. I was catching air, and lots of it. We had lunch together on the riverbank, and he gave me his hat. He called it a Clancy hat and said it was dripping with good luck and good fortune. He was right. Oh, I didn't catch any trout that afternoon, but I didn't slip headfirst into the cold river, either. The fellow from New Zealand did. He came up laughing, saying in that delightful down-under brogue that there weren't many rivers in the world that had given him a good dunking. He would always remember the Bullpasture, not only for its fish but also for its tricky footing.

Today, this stretch of the upper James is in a mild, easy mood, moving patiently past sweet-smelling forests.

Up ahead is a small section of riffles. Nothing cataclysmic, but that doesn't matter. Rapids, big or small, any rapids of whatever consequence, set a canoeist's blood racing and his temperature soaring. At first, I notice only a sound, a distant hissing like steam escaping. Closer, the character of the sound changes, intensifies, becomes a soft howl, as mournful as a coyote's cry. Standing in the green canoe, I study what is ahead. The rapids are small, despite their thumping sound, water-tossed waves swirling about large boulders near midstream, boulders worn smooth as glass by the ever-grinding water. Water is being drawn or sucked to the left, toward the stones. I paddle toward the right bank, then let the river's own energy and a few correcting strokes carry the canoe safely past the menacing stones shining in the light.

Below the rapids, the river is calm again, a series of deeper pools. The green canoe and I drift along, sharing the river's rhythms, its direction, its fate. We are on its time clock. There are no sounds save the wind among the trees, the liquid trill of moving water, bird songs from the deep woods. Few things can change life as drastically as a canoe. Floating in a canoe, time itself is different, not a flow of hours, but of geography and sunlight. A journey in a canoe down a fine river is an enduring enchantment, a memory greater than the passing years.

What other craft but a canoe can give you so much for so little? In design, the canoe is simple, practical, purposeful, graceful, unpretentious, and wholly useful. Nothing about a canoe is excess or frivolous. Canoes shyly hide their power, strength, and responsiveness behind unobtrusive, uncluttered lines. Canoes are a legacy of a time past when we were closer to the natural world, when rivers were our interstates, when we were more dependent on nature and in awe of it. Indeed, canoes remain a tangible remembrance and testimony of our former passion for mystery, discovery, and reckless adventure, a quenchless thirst for knowing what was beyond the next bend, down the next valley, over the next mountain.

I was lucky. I got to know canoes early. I was just a boy. That was an asset, however. My grandfather firmly believed that canoes are meant especially for the young. There is no engine to constantly tinker with, little upkeep, no fuel to buy. Canoes run splendidly with no fuss on equal portions of river and muscle. Canoes are spirited and almost never quit. They can float in an inch of water and on a thimbleful of desire. And should a river dry up or get too mean, a canoe doesn't mind a portage, a lift to where the water is more suitable. Portages only increase a canoeist's regard for his canoe and for floatable lakes and rivers. Canoes are not only the supreme means of river travel, but their uses are also inestimable. More than once, the old man and I used our canoes as shelter in pouring rain, as our dining table, even as swaying beds tied along the river on cool summer nights. If you looked after a canoe, the old man told me, it, in equal measure, would return the favor a hundredfold, just as this old green canoe drifting down the waters of the upper James does and has done again and again on so many rivers throughout the South.

(1987)

Permit Me This

An hour before dawn and already the sky to the east is luminescent, streaked with veins of soft oranges and deeper blues. The skiff rocks gently as the changing tide moves in over this shallow saltwater flat off the Florida Keys, slightly northwest of Pine Key. Tendrils of moonlight undulate on the water, and the wind blows onshore.

The guide holds the skiff at the edge of the flat where the bottom disappears in deeper water. The sun gains the horizon, sunlight spilling over the sea with the slow deliberation of lava flows.

The shallow bottom of the flat is not a fixed topography; rather, it is a landscape in constant motion, a chaos of blurred shadows, the wrinkling of life in perpetual motion. Tides feed these flats, nurture them, and in turn, lure the predators, those who risk the shallow water to feed on the flat's bounty of mollusks and crustaceans. Already, sunlight has flashed off the chain mail scales of a big tarpon rolling on the surface of the water, feeding hungrily. As the sun rises and the water warms, others will come; the munificent plenty of the flats is too great a temptation.

I study marine charts, marking our bearing just as sunlight glints off the tangled, reddish knots of mangrove roots that line the shore of the flat. There is no mistake: This is the place. I have circled it in red marker, bold and thick. It was here that I saw *Trachinotus falcatus*, or permit.

The guide calls them jacks, and it's true enough. Permits are but another fascinating member of the jack family. The waters off North America host more than thirty species of jacks, including the yellowtail, jack crevalle, and amberjack. Jacks are noted as ruthless fighters, fish of amazing endurance.

"Yeah, call 'em jacks," says the guide. "Better yet, call 'em ghosts." And we both laughed, a laugh mixed with as much frustration and vexation as exhilaration, for surely the permit is the most challenging game fish of the saltwater flats, a fish so elusive that the mere sight of one is cause for haunting piscatorial tales. Permit are simply vexing fish. Even when they are seen, even when an angler tempts them with his most alluring and enticing saltwater fly, few permit actually acknowledge the temptation, and still fewer are ever hooked. It is not that permit are that rare; indeed, there are days here on the flats off the Keys when anglers have spotted many feeding permit, enough to drive legions of saltwater fly-fishermen to sanity's edge. It's that they are so perplexing, beyond the hold of any fixed rules or definitions. It's not surprising then that sooner or later permit get to the saltwater angler, filling his daydreams and night dreams with images and glimpses that taunt and bewilder and rattle the nerves. The permit becomes more than just another fish. It assumes the aspect of a Moby Dick, that specter, that magnificent illusion, beautiful and maddening, that always breaks the line. The pools of light on the surface of the flat widen, and I watch the current, the moving water, how it highlights every detail of the shallow bottom, how it shapes every contour. Meanwhile, I rig up the G. Loomis IMX fly rod. It is 9 feet and throws a No. 9-weight forward line. Of late, it has had luck, taking bonefish and small tarpon. A man pursuing permit needs every grace fortune has to spare.

I hooked my last permit with a Loomis rod. It was working the bottom with its blunt snout, scaring up shrimp and crabs that were buried in the sand. I eased slowly, carefully out of the skiff, sure to keep my shadow away from the feeding fish, and moved with almost painful deliberation toward it. Each step closed the distance until I cast the line firmly forward letting the fly drop slightly to the right of its great head. The fish hung in the water like a bloated balloon for just an instance, then it came— that pressure on the line, a raw power, as if I had hooked and been hooked by some primordial force, by the heavy weight of evolution itself. A great fish it was, too, taking line like a bonefish, running the line down to the last foot or less on the reel time and again. It was a pandemonium of jerks and tugs, pulls and yanks, wrapping the line around every tuft of turtle grass and pinnacle of coral, then finally running for the tangle of mangrove roots as it flailed its body desperately on the bottom, determined to break loose. Which it did—and all in less than 30 seconds. As the tippet snapped, I noticed that I was on my knees, the fly rod high overhead, the saltwater of the flat joining with the sweat running down my face and hands and arms. As for the permit, it had vanished, yet another piscine shadow darting about my memory.

I remember; the permit does not. That is the difference between us, and I wonder sometimes who is actually the more fortunate creature. There are five species of permit, all of them perplexing. Larger permit favor the warm waters of South Florida, especially the Keys. Adult permit sport a blue-gray back that glints and flashes in the sun's glare, often seeming deep blue or polished ebony, depending on the sunlight's slant. Seen in profile, the permit's body is dull silver and looks as flat as a manhole cover. A thin piping of black on the tail fin and dorsal fin makes a tailing or feeding permit easy to identify once spotted. Too, permit will often feed in large schools. I have heard stories of ten to fifteen of them being seen at once on the same flat. Ironically, in my star-crossed years as an angler, the more permit I cast to on a flat, the less interested any seem to be in even acknowledging my humble offerings. Apparently, it is the lone permit, perhaps a bit nervous, a little more eager, that is most likely to consider a wider range of possible meals. Even so, no matter how deep their rapacious hunger, permit do not easily give in to the temptation of handsome saltwater flies, no matter how irresistible their apparent allure.

I drift in and out of daydreams, and the morning passes. Two bonefish flash off the skiff's bow working the tide, and a big ray drifts across the flat, just for an instant, seeming to float below the surface like a bolt of sodden black cloth cast to the fortunes of wind and sea. I ease into the water, and it is wonderfully cool against my skin compared to the hot, dry wind. At perhaps 40 feet from a bonefish, I cast my line, letting the wind take the fly, ease it naturally onto the surface. Even before the fly begins to sink, something about it gains the bonefish's interest: perhaps it is its size and shape or the way the light angles off it, or perhaps it is that slight motion that for a moment gave it animation as I stripped the line. Whatever the reason, the bonefish struck with power and tenacious resolve, emptying my reel to the backing in what seemed a matter of seconds, and still it ran. Only the friction and weight of the heavy fly line finally eclipsed its stamina. Even so, it continued fighting, lashing out each time I brought it near, each time I could make out the substance of its shadowy bulk, until it finally came close enough for me to lift gently to the surface, take the hook from its mouth, then slide it back into the water where I watched it regain its strength and swim eagerly for the deep water at the edge of the flat.

The guide sat on the deck dangling his feet in the cool water, and at last, I joined him. We ate the last of the Slim Jims and drank the last of the root beer. Just as the day's fading light gathered in shimmering pools across the glassy face of the flat, I saw it. It was that unmistakable silhouette of brooding power and raw wildness: a great permit moving out across the flat with the ebbing tide, moving away from the light into the safety of deep water, dark water.

"A ghost," mumbled the guide.

"Of course," I gasped. "Just another ghost."

(1989)

The Early Evening Rise

When we pull the truck off the old logging road by the wooden bridge, it is already late afternoon. Even so, the sun is still warm against our backs. Sunlight shimmers in the newly green forest that smells of hemlock and magnolia. Below the bridge in a small ravine, cucumber magnolias are in bloom, their flowers as big as greenish-yellow saucers.

We grab our gear from the truck: a fishing net, an 8-foot fly rod, an Orvis reel, an extra spool of line, some leaders and tippets. A handful of assorted flies are packed safely in a small metal case.

We walk upstream along the road and along the river. The sound of cascading water, clear and cold, rushing over smooth gray and brown stones, is calming, soothing. Up ahead, where the river bends, are the big boulders, big as trucks, between which are the large, quiet pools full of trout. By the time we reach what is called Richard's Pool, one of the largest along the river, the sun is off the water and glistens among the treetops. Leaves sparkle like Roman candles. Meanwhile, shadows begin to ease across the river. It is still and pleasant.

Now, it happens gradually, slowly, subtly. There are small swirls at the head of the largest of the pools. Trout are rising. We watch for a moment and do not cast. We wait, watching the fish, watching the hatching insects lifting off the surface of the water. We do not want to disturb what is happening. We do not want to suddenly end it. For a moment we are content just to watch. There are more swirls at the surface, more trout. We can clearly see the handsome shape and coloring of the brown trout rising.

We prepare carefully, tie on a caddis fly with a modified hangman's knot. The cast yields nothing, as does the second and the third. We stop for a minute, rest against one of the huge boulders at the edge of the pool, again just observing the evening rise. We clip off the caddis fly and take out our fly case to find a soft gray-backed stone fly. We tie the stone fly on. Just then another brown trout, weighing perhaps 2 pounds, jumps. There is a splash of green-blue water, then silence. We cast above the swirling water letting our line drift down over the feeding fish. Again, nothing. Another cast. Nothing once more. Thin shafts of soft, dying sunlight glimmer on the race of the river; shadows lengthen; the once brightly lit pool becomes shrouded in gray shadows. We snip off the stone fly and tie on an Adams, dipping it in the fly-drying solution.

Again, we cast above the hungrily feeding trout, letting the Adams drift naturally on the surface among them. This time there is a nudge, barely perceptible. We jerk the rod and line straight up in the air. There is a pull of weight at the end of the line, a fish pulling against us. The trout thrashes violently trying to throw the hook. Once it leaps from the water and lands in the pool on its side. We reel him in. He is a handsome brown trout, perhaps 2 pounds in weight. We touch him gently on the flank and let him go.

The rise of insect and trout continue, even intensify. The trout grow frantic. No light breaks through the canopy of the trees above, and the sun is low in the sky so that the day becomes a smudge of claret-colored light in the West. The shadows enveloping Richard's Pool grow thicker, darker. We groom our Adams, coat it again with drying solution so it will float on the surface of the pool well. Then we cast. This time an even bigger trout hits. It fights fiercely, diving for the deep water of the pool, then racing for the protection of the boulders. It takes more than five minutes for us to net him. He is as fine a brown trout as we have seen in years and weighs over 3.5 pounds.

As the light fades, we step out from the side of the boulders and stand at the edge of the big pool. Another cast and another strike, only this fish throws the hook almost immediately. It is now twilight, and the rise seems to reach its peak. So frantic are the trout feeding in the pool that the water of the usually calm pool seems to boil with their activity. With the sunlight gone from the surface of the pool, the trout, normally so nervous and skittish, have emerged from their secret holes and hiding places beneath the boulders to partake of the sudden insect feast.

Dusk and early morning, before the sun is high enough to burn off the shadows, is the time of day when most trout feed with little or no fear. For without the sun and its reflections, the trout have nothing above them but grayness and flat shadows and nothing to warn them of trouble. There are no silhouettes of dangers, impending or otherwise, nothing to frighten the fish. Even more important, during times of heavy shadow, trout are less able to distinguish color and form, so they are less picky and selective in their feeding habits. For this brief time, most trout will strike at just about anything, as long as it is more or less the right size and shape—as long as it resembles an insect that they feed on.

It is now past 6 PM, and we have taken and released eight trout on our No. 14 Adams. We also have gotten some with the same size stone flies and caddis flies. At 4:30 PM neither had worked, but by 6 PM the trout are taking them without hesitation.

We keep casting into the long, darkening shadows until we can no longer see our fly or even much of our bright-yellow line. Still, we cast one more time, letting the Adams float for a long time on the surface of the now quiet pool. As the sky goes from gray to black, the fish are gone. There are no more swirls on the surface of the pool, no further signs of hatching insects. The surface of the river, so busy with prowling fish and rising insects moments before, is now flat and still and looks like a mirror in a dimly lit room.

As familiar as we are with all the scientific findings, reasons, and explanations for the behavior of trout during an evening rise, as much as we believe and understand all this information, the moment we are actually there to watch and experience it seems somehow wild and magical. The

rise seems to express the very essence of trout fishing—
that blend of rod and reel, river and forest, wind and sky,
light and flowing water, fish and fisherman—that makes
fly fishing unique, special, an experience like no other. For
us, the evening rise is a little like the difference between
observing art and being a part of the artistic process. Being
caught up in it, the fisherman is all of a sudden no longer
simply a spectator, someone operating on the fringes of nature. Instead, he has become a part of the process, a link in
that ancient chain of sunlight, insect, river, and fish. The evening rise is an atavistic experience, and for a brief moment,
the fisherman is a part, a visual part, of the natural world in
a way that men rarely are these days.

After twilight, we gather up our gear, walk back down
the logging road toward the truck, thinking of the evening,
the swirling pool, the gorgeous trout, the light glistening
off the pool before dusk like starlight. Beside us, as we reach
the truck, the river runs on, a low roaring sound in the
darkness.

(1986)

GADGETS & GEAR

Outdoor Catalogs:
A Divertissement

I have not been sleeping well lately and have finally discovered the source of my malady: My bed is too far removed from my burgeoning collection of outdoor catalogs. During the long winter months when the trout won't rise and the quail won't fly, these catalogs are a tonic. Their colorful pages keep me at peace, level headed, and even tempered.

Outdoorsmen cling to such catalogs the way housebound gardeners browse wide-eyed through the latest seed catalogs, mentally sowing the soil, heralding in the distant spring. It is much the same for the downtrodden outdoorsman trapped inside by heavy weather in a house overflowing with the latest tantalizing and exotic offerings from L.L. Bean and Orvis. Such a condition is tantamount to having the showroom of the nation's largest outdoor emporium sprawled about one's den. The effect is something like malaria: a fever that won't go up or down, chills, nervous twitches, and an immediate, urgent impulse to fondle credit cards and memorize toll-free customer-service numbers.

Outdoor catalogs are unnerving, at least to the outdoorsman. The idea that so much exciting and wondrous gear is available beyond the doorway simply by picking up the telephone tends to make one giddy. Giddiness, in turn, quickly edges into outright addiction, an addiction that seems, in my case at least, to be hereditary. Outdoor catalogs got under my grandfather's skin as well. He was *truly* devoted to them. He received them by the dozens, read them again and again as if they were biblical gospel, collected them the way some people collect paper clips or baseball cards.

His condition, bad most of the year, collapsed altogether during the solitary winter months. He spent hours near the fireplace, paper and pencil in hand, poring over the latest catalogs. He would plan dangerous and thrilling fly-fishing trips to New Zealand or hunting trips to the Alaskan backcountry, canoe wild Canadian rivers, walk up ring-necked pheasants in spent Kansas cornfields. Day in and day out he walked the glossy aisles of the catalogs, a trout fisherman and upland bird hunter on a mad shopping spree, outfitting himself by mail. Each expedition required a special mix of gear and planning. The orders, each mounting to thousands of dollars, were never made, of course. They were the raw ingredients of his dreams, but he did make heavy practical use of the catalogs, those stapled pages displaying items to fit a sportsman's every need.

During the years I lived with him, hardly a month passed that the postman did not show up with some odd-looking package that turned out to be a new fly rod or reel, a thermal hunting coat or gun case, new neoprene waders, or perhaps a new assortment of handsomely tied, brightly colored dry flies imported from England.

The old man never got enough of outdoor catalogs. He would ponder them for hours on end without fatigue. And no matter what or how much he might buy, he always, in the end, seemed to be short one essential piece of gear. He never caught up. The catalog companies were always ahead of him, always coming up with something new and exciting and irresistible, whether it be a lighter and more responsive fly rod or a dog bed that promised Cody, his setter, comfort and happiness.

The catalogs arrived with a soothing regularity, like the seasons. The tasteful, slightly sentimental covers of the L.L. Bean catalog signaled fall's approach long before the trees did. Leafing through the shiny pages of coats and hats and warm wool shirts, my grandfather could feel a chill building in the air. Reading the catalogs—with their simple, direct, honest, even lighthearted prose—was like talking to a neighbor. It was a language that was hard to resist, even if the conversation did cost him.

As far as I know, my grandfather cherished no other mail, not even his tax refund, as much as he did the outdoor catalogs. He waited their arrival with a cheerful impatience, and when they did show up in the mailbox, he would begin to mark in pencil all his wants, wishes, desires, and dreams.

Next to the outdoors itself, the catalogs were his truest happiness and greatest weakness. Once inside the alluring pages of the catalogs, the old man lost all sense of reserve and restraint and became wonderfully irrational. Just being around him was a heady experience. He was always buying the most exotic pieces of equipment. There was one occasion, for instance, when he bought something called stream cleats (picture snow chains for wading boots), even though he never knew exactly what they were or how to use them. When they arrived, he put them in a closet already packed with unused bizarre items of outdoor gear. As far as I know, he never used the cleats, but just having them nearby, I suppose, eased his mind. He was a man who believed in fortune, and he never knew when he might have the opportunity to crawl over slippery moss-covered stones in his stream cleats to sneak up on a 5-pound rainbow trout hiding in a shallow river pool.

Anyway, I have moved *my* outdoor catalogs to the table next to my bed. I feel better, calmer. I have just ordered five-hundred duck decoys for next season, even though the swamp where I hunt ducks barely has room for fifty decoys. Who knows? Maybe next year the water will rise. Anyway, these decoys are special. They are guaranteed. The catalog says so.

(1989)

Talkin' Turkey

I first met Allen Jenkins at 4:30 in the morning at his home outside Liberty, Mississippi. Allen's house sits on a modest Mississippi hill above his place of business, the M.L. Lynch Company. Lynch is probably the most venerable name in the increasingly competitive world of wild turkey calls. The Lynch box calls have become synonymous with the finest traditions of Southern turkey hunting. Each box call is handmade (going through more than seventy steps) of the best and most resonant wood, mahogany. Allen went to work for Mr. Lynch at twenty-two, when the calls were made in the basement of the Lynch home in Birmingham. When Allen took over the business a few years later, he moved it to Mississippi.

At five o'clock we leave, shadows wrapped in darkness. The trip is a short one. Allen leases a nice piece of piney woods not far from his office. He is a lucky man—his business is also his passion.

As soundless as a breeze, Allen enters the woods. Almost everything he wears or carries, save his shotgun, he has designed and made. His mind runs on a steady flow of innovation. The camouflage turkey-hunting vest is his idea. It has more pockets than a fly-fishing vest. Turkey hunters believe in pockets. Each pocket is a new potential, a new possibility, even if it's packed only with luck. The pockets of Allen's vest carry an incredible assortment of handmade Lynch calls. He is a walking warehouse of delightful sounds, wild sounds, primitive sounds.

Perhaps 10 paces behind a tangled thicket, we sit on camouflage pads, our backs to a comfortable oak near the edge of an open field. Silent, motionless, we sit in a steady drizzle. In such discomfort, a turkey hunter finds happiness. Harder rain and mud would only increase our pleasure. A turkey hunter needs something insidious to blame his lack of success on. Turkey hunting can weaken a man's resolve and happiness. It is not for the meek, the optimistic, the faint of heart, or the impatient. Once addicted, the turkey hunter becomes obsessed with outsmarting turkeys. It's more than a matter of pride; it's a matter of dignity. Indeed, fooling turkeys becomes almost as important as doing them in. Consequently, turkey hunters go to great lengths to get the best of this quizzical creature.

Matching wits with a wild turkey first requires that the modern turkey hunter become invisible. This he does by dressing himself in a dreary mix of camouflage from head to toe. This idea is to look like just another lichen

-mottled tree stump or an unassuming bush, one that is mobile and heavily armed. Some turkey hunters complete the disguise by painting their faces, dressing their shotguns in camouflage sleeves, and even donning camouflage boots and gloves. When turkey season opens, nothing in the woods is as it appears to be.

Allen and I sit in the rain against the tree well past dawn. The woods are cold and gray. He has tried four calls, producing a lovely quartet of whispered clucks and yelps that drift through the woods like a damp fog. But the love songs go unanswered; if there's a turkey out there, he is warm and dry and a bird of cold emotions.

A gobbler is a lot harder to find than he is to kill. A wild turkey is a master woodsman. In a world of sense and sensation, he is a raw nerve. Even the rustle of a leaf upsets him. What the turkey cannot hear, he can see, and what he cannot run from, he can fly from. No two share the same virtues or vices. None have the same quirks or habits. The only consistent thing about them is their inconsistency.

Late in the morning, Allen is sitting in the big chair behind his desk. Down the hall is the constant yelp and cackle of turkey calls. The M.L. Lynch Company employs twenty people full time and still has to struggle to meet the demand for calls. For the third time in an hour, Allen leaps from the chair, runs down the hall. He has heard a call he doesn't like. The sound isn't true. He works on it for ten minutes. Still dissatisfied, he dumps the disappointing call in the reject pile. "Quality is *it* when it comes to turkey calls," he says. "The birds get smarter every year. They're not dumb enough to come to just any squeal."

Calling turkeys is not extremely difficult, especially when compared to the heartache involved in finding the turkeys. The spring call is essentially a love song, a gentle amorous note that hangs in the air like a whispered invitation. And if there is one thing a mature gobbler cannot abide, it is an unattached female.

Technology has infiltrated turkey hunting just like everything else, but with less success. Although most turkey hunters will try any call, no matter how eccentric, sooner or later most return to what is enduring and reliable. For many of them that means a drawer of Lynch boxes, a good Williams wingbone, a good peg, and a well-rubbed piece of slate.

Allen makes excellent calls for many reasons, not the least of which is his nearly perfect sense of sound and pitch. I know of only two other turkey hunters that can equal Allen when it comes to a keen ear for turkey talk. One is Lovett Williams; the other is Lamar Williams. Both men are from Florida and are unrelated.

Lovett Williams is a wildlife biologist. He worked for the State of Florida and is largely responsible for the comeback of the Florida turkey (a subspecies of the eastern turkey). He now divides his time between managing Fisheating Creek Hunting Lodge near Palmdale and writing about turkeys. One of his books is *The Voice and Vocabulary of the Wild Turkey,* which deals in detail with every utterance the turkey makes, what it means, and how the hunter should respond to it. It's the closest a turkey hunter is likely to get to actually breaking a gobbler's code.

Lamar Williams makes Widowmaker Turkey Calls in his home in Starke, Florida. All his calls are known for their quality and craftsmanship, but Lamar is perhaps best known as the most talented wingbone callmaker now working in the South. His wingbones are as much art as craft, finely turned instruments that produce a vibration, a sound that a spring gobbler finds hard to ignore. Williams's handmade box calls are also among the very best, producing a full range of sounds. Like Lynch boxes, the craftsmanship is exquisite, telling in every detail.

What each of these educated and wise turkey hunters and observers seems to agree on is that less is best. A turkey hunter doesn't need a vest full of calls, when two or three will see him through. "Softness is the key," says Jenkins. "Too many hunters sound like a church organ with all the stops open. In the spring, gentle clucks and tree yelps work best— nothing too harsh, nothing bold, nothing too aggressive. Once you've called, wait." Patience is the turkey's undoing; excitement is the hunter's. One call may rouse a turkey; two made in haste will surely frighten him. If nothing happens in ten or twenty minutes, try a sweet melody of ruffled purrs and yelps or a little cutting (a series of louder, impatient clucks). If a blue head the size of a baseball hasn't popped up like a periscope near you in half an hour either move on or go to the last resort, a challenge—resounding, cackling gobble made by taking a box call and shaking the lid vigorously back and forth over the box. In the lexicon of turkeys, this is the same as throwing down the gauntlet. If the gobbler doesn't acknowledge the insult, the hunter is left with two choices: return to the hunt or take a nap.

After much work I have simplified my life. I now own only a handful of turkey calls—my irreplaceable Williams wingbone and a dozen of the best old boxes, half Lynch and half Williams, and Lovett Williams's indispensable turkey-calling cassette tapes. Even so armed, I know the turkeys, as always, still have the upper hand, just as I know that the old wingbone in my pocket is the only magic I have to make the feathered ghosts I pursue take momentary shape.

(1988)

An Angler's Lament

In anticipation of the warm months to come, I have been busy checking my fishing equipment, straightening up my tackle box, cleaning rods and reels. This morning, like a boat captain calling his first fire drill, I hastily put on all my fishing gear and stood boldly in front of the mirror. I looked like a soldier ready for combat, armed with enough equipment to see me through any siege. I felt silly. I looked ridiculous. It seems that no matter what I do toward simplifying my fishing life, I am determined to bog down trout fishing in endless theories of technique, pounds of gear and paraphernalia—in short, make it more complicated than it needs to be.

I was doing nicely as a trout fisherman, getting out of the house, frittering away my time walking and canoeing some of the most beautiful trout rivers and streams in the South. I even caught fish. Not a lot of fish, but enough.

After all, in trout fishing, it is not really the fish that matter, it is the experience, that almost-mystical relationship man has with rod and artificial insect and trout and rivers. Enough for anyone you might think? I was happy, at ease, content—or so I thought. But then I got into my thirties and got nervous and threw contentment aside. I signed up to attend a trout-fishing school—three days of intense, unending exposure to the latest techniques in casting and in the massive growth of technology that seems to be absorbing the sport of trout fishing.

These days, it seems, a trout fisherman needs a good deal more than a trout stream, fly rod, and a fairly decent fly to catch trout. He must have waders. Oh, not just any waders, but ones made of feather-light nylon, complete with special wading boots and socks—price, $160. If the rivers he fishes are not chest deep, then he must have hip boots—price, $80. A good pair of tennis shoes and a pair of shorts, the poor man's waders, are simply out of the question. Evidently, no trout worth its pedigree will take a fly from a fisherman decked out in such common garb, no matter what he is presenting, dainty dry fly or a juicy night crawler. Too, today's successful fly fisherman must have a snappy-looking fly fisherman's vest—price, $70. The vest, of course, will not work if empty. Every pocket must be cheerfully filled. Empty pockets translate into a barren hook, ever fishless.

Last spring I rested on the bank of the Linville River in North Carolina and for an hour took a quick inventory of the gear I have been toting about to Southern trout streams for years. My fishing vest was a thing of wonder, armed to the teeth. It still is. There is one adjustable flexible flashlight—$17. I tried using it one year during an evening swirling rise of insects on the Bullpasture River in Virginia. It didn't work. It didn't work for months thereafter until my son suggested rather smugly that I try putting batteries in it. In one of my vest's twenty pockets, I have an ingenious little walking stick that breaks down into sections and, with a flick of the wrist, unfolds to become a 50-inch walking staff—price, $50. I wish I knew which pocket it is in. I could have used it on the Rapidan River in Virginia when I kept slipping on the river's glasslike, moss-covered stones, producing loud splashes that scared me and the trout both. I have a handy trout net that set me back $50. I have been tangled up in it more times than any trout. Now the netting is torn and in disarray. It hangs from a D-ring on the back of my trout vest and catches all of the limbs, twigs, shrubs, and branches I somehow manage to miss while casting.

Somewhere in my vest is a handsome fish-weighing scale—$30. It will weigh fish up to 15 pounds, 4 ounces. I have not used it in years, mostly because all my trout seem to be undernourished and refuse to tip the scale in any direction. Always at my side is my Orvis Arctic Creel. It works like a desert water bag. The creel is soaked in water, which in turn keeps the trout cool—if you catch any, that is.

Pinned to the front of my fishing vest is a large knife. This is to cut me free of the 20-pound vest should I suddenly become less than buoyant. The front of my vest is also decorated with a pair of nail clippers, an instrument of execution used to remove lackadaisical flies that shrink from their duty of luring trout. The clippers are rustproof and cost $12.50. Next to the clippers is a pair of surgical forceps used for daintily and skillfully removing the hook from caught fish. These forceps allow for a quick-and-painless surgery, at least for the trout, of which I keep fewer and fewer these days because they are just too precious. Tucked away in one of these pockets is a $6 hook sharpener I plan on using just as soon as I start catching fish.

Too, there is a bottle of superfloat guaranteed to keep my dry flies well groomed and afloat. Dry flies are questionable swimmers and are easily drowned. And if the trout are being particularly uncooperative, not biting on the surface at all, I have a special bottle of mud, a little dab of which will cause my leader and attached nymph to sink just below the river's surface, there to perform a dance no trout can withstand.

I have a $2 thermometer in a top pocket of the vest. This I keep near at hand at all times to take each stream's temperature as well as my own. I seem to run a slight fever whenever I am around trout. One pocket of the vest is permanently reserved for a knot-tying tool, $10, because barrel knots, nail knots, cinch knots, and the like are anything but a cinch, at least for me.

And there is more: four packets of tippets, other leaders, and an extra reel of sinking fly line. And spread everywhere, in almost every pocket, stuck to the vest, my shirt, and my hat are flies, perhaps five dozen of them at an average cost of $1.50 per fly. I have handfuls of Green Drake Wulffs and Grey Wulffs, Pale Evening Duns and Dark Hendricksons, Light Cahills and Adams of every size, dainty March Browns and milky-white Cream Variants, jazzy-looking feathered beetles, mock grasshoppers and ants, a nice assortment of nymphs, those delicate, flashy streamers, and moody stoneflies.

In a good season I use perhaps ten. I always try the Adams first, no matter what the trout appear to be feeding on, because with the Adams I catch trout. Trout, at least Southern trout, just dote on the Adams dry fly. I have seen them stop eating everything from June bugs to sculpins to take an Adams that has the gall to come drifting by.

So here I sit waiting for another season with more than a $1,000 worth of the latest and most advanced trout-fishing gear, the very epitome of man's ingenuity. Still the trout outwit me, get the best of me. Trout are not like bass: they never cooperate. There is just no figuring trout. You would think, after all, that a fisherman armed with this much equipment, with this much technical superiority, would have the upper hand. You would think the trout would give it up, throw up their fins and surrender peacefully. Not so. I suspect this next trout season will be like the last and that the trout will go on treating my handsome, noble flies like second-class citizens. They will completely ignore them, treat them as insults to the fare provided them by the natural world. But I go on, and at the rate I am going, trout are quickly taking on the value of filet mignon—worth, for this weary fisherman at least, in the neighborhood of $100 a pound.

But, finally, it does not matter. Among fish, trout are a luxury, beautiful prima donnas worth every trick, bit of tomfoolery, gadget, and deceit it might take to hook one. It's exciting to feel its power and grace, however briefly, before removing the hook, gently nudging its iridescent flanks, watching it return to the deep pool or the fast water of a mountain stream, the world where it inexorably belongs.

And as for me, perhaps this next season I will slip off the waders, slip on my shorts and tennis shoes, and tie a No. 14 Adams. I will settle back, take whatever splendor and trout the days might bring.

(1987)

Classic Cane

(This story appeared in Fly Rod & Reel *in 1989, under the nom de plume Churchill Payne, which, according to Harry's widow, is one of several pen names he used throughout his writing career. This piece contains references to characters and places central to his masterpiece,* The Earth is Enough, *which appeared that same year.)*

I grew up in a household of men. There was my grandfather, my uncle Albert, and me. With the absence of women and the farm's consistent poor showing, we happily devoted ourselves to fly fishing and the exasperating pursuit of trout. The life suited us, and the old men refused to abandon it. Whatever their shortcomings, both remained lifelong piscatorial monogamists, each singularly devoted to the life that was and is fly fishing. For them, the most satisfying aspect of that life was the at once vexing and pleasurable art of taking trout solely on a handmade bamboo rod.

Neither of these Southern highlanders fit the accepted image of a dapper and sophisticated fly fisherman. To them, fly fishing was not a right of birth but a blessing, an elegant luxury in an often hard and despairing existence. Fly fishing assumed a grand stature in their lives. It was no more a mere hobby, a sport, or a pastime than was a man's religion. Indeed, as far as these old men knew, the noble trout and the lithe bamboo rod were as close to things divine as they were likely to reach. High-mountain trout streams whispered the good word of the gospels. Fickle trout rose, leaving them with unforgettable sermons, and each man stood knee-deep, his little bamboo rod his staff, his link to a nearer, more immediate, and more accessible heaven. Not long before my uncle Albert died at the age of ninety-two, we were fishing on Arkansas's lovely White River. At noon we relaxed on a gravel bar, eating hardboiled eggs and drinking root beer. In the White's ubiquitous lacy fog we looked like gray shadows. All of a sudden, the old man spoke. He talked of fly fishing, which was uncommon. He'd been a man who liked to fish for trout rather than speak of them. As he talked, he wiped dry the guides of his little bamboo rod, an aged Paul H. Young that was dark as rubbed wild cherry bark and limber as a length of willow. He liked fly fishing, he said softly, because it had backbone and character. And class. If it provided the practitioner regular disappointment, so did it yield unexpected excitement and elation, and enough solitude to ease any man's troubled spirit. For more than seventy years he had cast a fly, and there had been no boredom or lack of challenge. Each cast, he said, had given him a sense of renewal as deep and real as any emotion he had ever experienced, including matrimony—another subject on which he had considerable knowledge, for he had outlived five wives. He admitted that the angling life had its own special miseries, and noted that trout fishermen carried on by developing selective memories. They survived by lingering on only the most enriching moments of their fly-fishing lives—the wild and beautiful rivers, the always haunting trout, the remarkable rods and reels, each taut line and the inexpressible joy of a sudden wildness hooked at the end of a line. Surely fly fishing, though both fickle and sincere, is a vital pursuit, as stimulating as a jolt of electric current; but a journey of consequence that is all beginnings and no end.

That fine day on the White, Uncle Albert said that a fly fisherman casts all his life for the secrets of rivers and of the trout they hold. He hooked few of either and so the allure was never diluted or tarnished.

It seemed fitting to Albert and my grandfather that things as mercurial as fly fishing and trout should employ chiefly a quixotic little rod fashioned from, of all things, a bizarre, woody, tree-like semitropical grass from Southeast Asia called bamboo. Bamboo rods were common in their day and did not yet have the reputation of being playthings of the rich, handsome, and expensive angling artifacts. These modest high-mountain farmers never fished with anything else. Albert particularly loved to discuss the wonders of the bamboo rod. He relished conversations about bamboo so he could haul out one of his favorite angling quotes, a line from Gervase Markham: "The Angler must entice, not command his reward." In short, a decent fly fisherman would not dare horse in a stream trout on anything but a bamboo rod and the lightest possible tackle. Angling for trout demanded a dose of the trout's own character—finesse, grace, subdued power. A bamboo rod.

Albert and my grandfather trusted in fate, and fate had been kind to them—as anglers, anyway. They'd spent their manhood in the years of the great American bamboo-rod triumvirate, the age of Hiram Leonard, Everett Garrison, and Jim Payne. These craftsmen, and others like E.C. Powell, F.E. Thomas, and Paul Young, were not mere rod makers, they were dedicated artisans who worked during a time when the heritage, traditions, and techniques of American fly fishing demanded nothing short of excellence.

Even when such rods were selling for $50 to $80, few average fly fishermen could afford a Leonard or even a Payne, for this was nearly a fifth of the farm's annual earnings. But in those years money did not deny bamboo's elusive magic, its beauty and its performance to any angler, for not only were there Leonards and Youngs and Paynes, so were there Grangers, Heddons, and Phillipsons, each a sound bamboo rod for a modest price. Albert had two Phillipsons, a Paramount, and a Paragon. Later he added a Granger Registered. Bamboo rods were much like his grouse dogs: he struggled to spread his time and affection among them equally.

On and off the river, both men spent hours with the handsome rods. There was great pleasure to be had just from handling them, feeling their grace and subtle strength, their coiled excitement.

Albert died in 1965. He was ninety-two. I was twelve. A month before he died he gave me his Phillipson Premier. Holding it in my hand, I thought it was as delicate as a reed, surely too frail to land even the smallest trout. At first I hung it on the wall, and felt guilty because I remembered Albert's theory on rods: "They die if you don't use 'em. They need the pull of fish to keep 'em fit and healthy."

I still have the old Phillipson. Unlike Albert, my grandfather, and me, it seems ageless. Sure, I've had it dressed up here, groomed there, but for the most part it's the same rod it was forty years ago. Bamboo rods are among those inanimate objects that soak up time and memories. It even has the feel of imbued motion and experience. In a world choking with objects, the Phillipson is a rare possession, one that endures with taste, one that still functions with the alacrity and promise of youth while it testifies to the fly-fishing life Albert led, a life of charm and quiet dignity.

Bamboo rods of whatever vintage, rods of quality and simple beauty, continue to make such statements, homilies that say today's fly fisherman can still believe in mystery and enchantments, as well as the modern cornucopia of angling science and technology.

Bamboo rods began to slip from favor in the 1950s as fly fishing began to fall under the spell of technology—especially the new materials that promised cheaper yet better fly rods. To a great extent the promises came true, and bamboo slid into hard times. First came fiberglass and then the angling revelation known as graphite. Although bamboo rods were pronounced obsolete, purists and romantics refused to allow their complete extinction. As the new wonder rods moved to the fore, bamboo, always the refined gentleman, settled back to become a classic of American fly-fishing heritage and lore. And then suddenly the bamboo was not only still an excellent, if underrated, fly rod, it became a hotly sought collectible and an astounding investment.

Graphite rods are "affordable," yes, but like a reliable yet average car, they begin to lose value the instant they are purchased. Meanwhile, the little bamboo rods, each a unique statement of angling knowledge and craftsmanship, appreciate steadily, old and new alike. Some rods that brought $50 were by the late '60s being sold for $1,500. Today the same rod, say, a wonderful Young Midge, might bring $3,000.

Debate over the merits of bamboo versus graphite is futile. In the end, both have their place in fly fishing. Graphite is, in many cases and particularly beyond the eight-foot mark, lighter, stronger, and powerful enough to produce very long casts. Graphite rods are practical and sturdy. Unlike bamboo, they demand no intimate attention to cure. A fly fisherman can own all the graphite rods he likes without getting too involved with any of them. Too, the immense new interest in and growth of fly fishing owes much to graphite and to those companies who make the best, the most pleasing of the graphite rods.

My grandfather owned several good graphite rods. He liked them fine, but he often said that he "couldn't feel fly fishing in them." For him only bamboo held that almost-magical touch, that fit so much like a soothing embrace. There is some truth in the old man's words. You cannot feel an individual craftsman's 40 to 80 hours of painstaking labor in an "advanced composite materials" rod. As yet, they don't have the mark of heritage. For those who have fished and caught trout on both rods, the question comes down to personal satisfaction, what the rod leaves them with. Among lovers of the bamboo rod there is the sense that a trout caught on bamboo is caught forever, held firmly in the imagination.

Since the '50s, minor bamboo-rod revivals have swept the fly-fishing community. Lately, though, it seems that a genuine bamboo renaissance has taken hold. More craftsmen, companies, and individuals, are making bamboo rods than at any time in the last half-century. There may be nearly 100 bamboo-rod builders working away at dimly lit workbenches throughout the country.

These bamboo revivals, says Tom Dorsey of Thomas & Thomas, makers of high-quality graphite and bamboo fly rods, are cyclical, coming between highs of technological innovation. "They seem to show up whenever fly fishermen begin to long for the simpler, less complicated aspects of the sport." Dorsey sees an analogy between fly fishermen and upland bird gunners. The bird hunter, after years of maturing, graduates from the automatic shotgun to the classic side-by-side, the hallmark of his sport.

"It's like that for the serious fly fisherman, too" says Dorsey. "Sooner or later, he will discover the romance and magic of bamboo, and will probably own one. Or want to own one. And he'll learn about its place in history, and that will enrich his fly fishing." After all, it is the bamboo fly rod that is fly fishing's magic wand, the keeper of so many of trout fishing's delightful secrets.

Dorsey finds it difficult to judge the volume and intensity of the new interest in bamboo because at Thomas & Thomas they rarely catch up on rod orders. "You can say," he muses, "that the bamboo fly rod has never really stopped. Let's face it, you can travel the same distance in a Toyota or a Jaguar—and no one *needs* the Jaguar. The question is, which one would you *rather* travel in, considering, naturally, that you can afford to make the choice? It's pretty much the same dilemma with some fly fishermen and bamboo rods."

While graphite continues to lead the technological revolution in rod material, it has replaced bamboo no more than Velcro has replaced shoelaces, buttons, and snaps. Indeed, many fly fishermen believe that today's bamboo rods are as good, perhaps even better, than the classics.

Todd Young constantly strives for improvement, which is quite a burden. The Paul H. Young rod company has been crafting outstanding bamboo fly rods for seventy-eight years. Paul Young, Todd's grandfather, almost singlehandedly changed the character of American fly fishing by the introduction of his Midge rod, back in the middle years of this century. With the Midge, fly fishing became a contest of intelligence and craft and the lightest possible tackle against the raw, wild power and cleverness of trout. Although it might cost him considerable profit (though his rods begin at $800), Todd maintains the quality and integrity of each and every Young rod, no matter the consequences. All of his time and energy go into his craft. He attends no fishing shows. He does not advertise. He has no need. Fly fishermen are drawn to excellence, "We have all the work we can handle and maintain the craftsmanship," he says in a firm voice.

Todd Young is serious about what he does: "The work is hard, sometimes tedious. Only a craftsman, a bamboo rod craftsman, could love it. Given the hours put into each rod—say, 50 hours, at least—I don't make much money. None of the best bamboo rod makers do. It's simply a love of craft, wanting to keep the best of American fly fishing alive, intact. This is not to say that graphite is without merit. It has its place, especially in the salmon and steelhead and saltwater rods, the big rods. For river and stream trout, though, the casting and presentation advantages all belong to bamboo."

Dangers accompany all revivals, even those as innocent as the renewed interest in bamboo. Given the substantial value of bamboo rods, old and new, poorly made rods are showing up. "Cheap imitations," Young calls them, with a craftsman's sincere disdain. The trend toward inexpensive, poorly crafted bamboo fly rods genuinely worries makers committed to excellence. "I see these horrible rods everywhere," says Young. "Cheap cane, sloppy, visible seams, loose fittings, substandard guides, ferrules, reel seats. On and on." The warning is obvious and simple: Beware. Never buy a rod you cannot examine, touch, feel, cast. Cheap bamboo is cheap forever.

There are many outlandishly expensive rods as well. Still, there is plenty of middle ground. For the angler who is patient and willing to look around, there are good bamboo rods to fit nearly every budget. The fly fisherman of today has more choice in bamboo rods than ever before. There are Todd Young's rods, and those of Thomas & Thomas. The R.L. Winston Company, in Twin Bridges, Montana, still makes a good bamboo fly rod, as does Orvis. There are rods crafted by individual builders like the renowned Hoagy Carmichael, Jr., that might cost as much as $2,000. All good rods. But there are also some, such as those made under the careful eye and exacting standards of longtime rodmaker Paul Hightower, at Bob's Rod & Tackle in Denver, that are not as expensive and yet have that special touch to them, that patina of heritage and tradition, that mark of quality and excellence—that tactile sensation that says there's fly fishing in this rod.

"My rods are nothing fancy," says Hightower. "But they're good rods and will give any angler a feel for the character of fly fishing with bamboo." Hightower should know. He, too, has spent a lifetime shaping bamboo, working for both Granger and Phillipson.

"I'm still making Phillipson rods," he says, "and trying to improve them, always. I keep at it for the same reason every bamboo rodmaker does: I want to make fly rods the way they're supposed to be made. The only difference is that I believe that quality *affordable* bamboo fly rods can be made." Hightower rods start at about $300.

Behind me, on the middle shelf of the bookcase, rests Uncle Albert's Phillipson. Just as Paul Hightower said, it's nothing fancy, but I know that if I take it down, let it rest for just a moment in my hand, I will recognize that unique touch, that sensation that says class and heritage and craftsmanship, that honest feel of bamboo that says fly fishing, whether its name is Leonard or Young, Thomas & Thomas, or Carmichael.

(1989)

WINGS, WIND & WONDER

Song of the Whippoorwill

Blue shadows at evening. Cold blue. Winter blue, pure and flawless, mottled shadows spreading across the rolling mountain fields. Everywhere, a sea of subtle light. As has been his habit for so many, many years, Silas Hobson puts on his heavy coat, wool cap, and gloves and leaves by the farmhouse's back door to walk the woods that bound his fallow fields. It is perhaps an hour before nightfall.

Many call Silas Hobson a silly old man. How foolish to be out trodding about in the cold looking for signs of change, listening to the wind, reading in it portents of the future. Yet there is as much logic to his wanderings as solace, as much knowledge as yearning. And why not. The natural world is a giddy gossip, full of news, rumor, intrigue. The allure of the woods is forever tempting, and Silas Hobson refuses to resist. As the mountain fields wait the thaw, the cut of his plow, the warming sun, he walks the deep-purple shadows along Plum Creek. And soon enough the old man hears it and is not disappointed. The whippoorwill's song. Such a plaintive voice; such a brooding song.

On hearing the bird, Silas Hobson, as always, goes no farther, but stays seated near the creek's edge on a great slab of ashen-gray granite, a stone the size of an old Cadillac. Although Silas Hobson admires all that is wild, all that is of the natural world, he has a special fondness for the whippoorwill, its strong character, its tenacity, its subtle boldness. How brash an act for a bird to sing such heady notes on such a raw day, the cold sunlight dissolving quickly. Its song is not so much a song at all, really, but just the noise of life.

Whippoorwills have been his neighbors on the land, a land that is theirs more than his. They are birds that are easy to like, admire. Whippoorwills are birds of the open countrysides, birds that need densely wooded hillsides and hollows, shrub-choked thickets, and the element of safety.

Whippoorwills are not members of a large or extended family of birds. They are night jars or goatsuckers, a rather small branch of avian genealogy. An old myth that whippoorwills, silent prowlers of the night, somehow managed to drink the milk of goats and cattle, left them with the name goatsuckers. Night jar, a more haunting and mysterious moniker, comes from these birds' often loud and unnerving night songs, sounds that truly seem to jar, unhinge the night hours.

True to their family upbringing, nightjars are all lovers of twilight, the darkness. Silas Hobson knows the whippoorwill singing across Plum Creek is the common Eastern whippoorwill, a bird that ranges freely and widely from Manitoba, Canada, south to Mississippi, Alabama, Georgia, northern Louisiana, and then east from North Dakota to Kansas to parts of South Carolina. Come winter, the great majority of Eastern whippoorwills will move South, follow the warming sun to the Carolinas and the Gulf Coast and even into Central and South America. For some reason, though, a few always elect to stay behind, face the winter and the cold, fight the hunger and misery with their mournful song. Indeed, there is evidence that some actually hibernate.

In size, whippoorwills are hardly startling birds. They are average, if that, being from 7 to 13 inches long and with a wingspan that can stretch to 19 inches. One of the qualities that Silas Hobson finds so delightful about whippoorwills is that despite their song, they are officially, scientifically, not proper songbirds. Almost everything about the whippoorwill is curious, a slap at reason. Even when trying to be polite, it is hard to describe their looks as other than quizzical. They are marked by rather flat heads, small bills, dark eyes, gaping mouths, and perhaps the most cryptic collage of plumage sported by any bird.

While awkward on the ground, the whippoorwill displays a great deal of grace on the wing. In flight, it is smooth, swift, making no more noise than a moth. On the wing, whippoorwills are easily distinguished from their cousins the nighthawks by their shorter, rounded wings and the egg-white wing patches of the male whippoorwills as they dart about the evening shadows feeding hungrily.

Whippoorwills feed on the wing and are proficient, deadly hunters, scooping up mouthful after mouthful of insects as they patrol the night skies. Once on the wing, they hunt in silence, hardly rustling the air. In moonlight, they flash by as a brownish blur.

As he sits on the big rock and thinks about it, Hobson cannot recall seeing but a few whippoorwills in full daylight—and those had been driven from their shadowy daytime cover. No, they always come at dusk, moving with the shadows, sailing low to the ground like excited woodcocks.

There is bounty in the night sky, at least for the whippoorwill and its kind, a feast of cutworms, potato beetles, grasshoppers, gnats, luna moths, mosquitoes, crickets, tent caterpillars, and moths. Silas Hobson always welcomes the presence of the whippoorwills because he knows that they eat more mosquitoes in a week than a purple martin eats in a lifetime.

On the ground, far back in the dappled shadows, just before taking wing, whippoorwills often produce a soft clucking sound not unlike that made by a chicken. Besides their persistent, repetitive call, this is perhaps the most distinctive sound they make. During the evening hours, whippoorwills seldom rest, but when they do, they prefer a branch or limb that is free of obstruction, open to the sky, the moon, and stars overhead. There is an allure, a tug between moonlight and whippoorwills. Nothing brings on their call in such strength and power as a rising full moon. If there is great joy in the whippoorwill's call, so is there great exasperation and even annoyance. Scientists who keep track of such things tell us that when it comes to calling, singing, whippoorwills don't usually get into full voice until between the hours of 2 AM and dawn. But each whippoorwill keeps its own schedule and calls whenever moved to do so, regardless of the laws of science.

Hobson listens intently to the bird across the creek. Its call is broken, sporadic, not like the great rhythmic calls of the spring when the valley would echo with the bird's nightly romancing—"whip-po-or-will . . . whip-poor-will," or the corrupted whistle, "chuck-rhip-ooor-eee." The noisy spring would soon give way to the quieter days of summer, the days of heavy feeding when there was less time for song or other diversions. Then the first cold days of autumn and they would call again, for many the last call before moving farther South, a retreat from the mountain cold. Hobson listens quietly and wonders why this bird has stayed behind. He does not know but is glad the bird has stayed for he enjoys his nightly company.

In spring, when in fine and full voice, a whippoorwill can produce one call per second. As a younger man, Silas Hobson had often counted the calls of the whippoorwills, marveling at their stamina. One bird called out its name fifty times, another seventy-five. The most calls he had ever counted from a single bird was 103 straight. That was the only night he could ever remember wishing that a whippoorwill would pack up, move on, do its courting outside some other man's window.

The night is getting colder, and the old man can feel it numbing his hands and feet. A harder wind blows down from the mountains, stinging his face. Again, the stubborn bird across the creek calls, and the old man smiles for it is a good sound, a fair song, a song of March and warmer winds.

(1989)

The Rising Bass

A chilly mist hung low over the small lake, drifting slowly over the water and through the dense woods that lined the shore. As the morning moved through the woods, the mist began to break up and evaporate like clouds of rising steam. The banks of the lake were thick with stands of bulrush and cattail reeds. Already the new spring had taken a firm hold among the cattails.

Where the cattails ended, the lake deepened, its bottom changing from dark mud to soft silt and small gravel with vast stretches of muted green underwater gardens of hornwort, tape grass, water milfoil, and pondweed. At the lake's edge, stood great oaks and maples, birch trees, willows, and sycamores, even a few hardy walnut trees. On mornings such as this—quiet, still, and nearly windless— the lake's smooth, unwrinkled surface was like an artist's canvas, a detailed portrait of the dark woods just beginning to turn silver green.

A handsome largemouth bass flicked his great tail, moved out of the dark shadows under the old wooden pier, worked his way along the lake's shallows not far from shore. Perhaps an hour after sunrise, he had taken a small snake as it moved out from the cover of the cattails. There was no struggle. He took the snake before the snake even knew he was in danger. His great hunger momentarily appeased, he moved now with less urgency, driven by his insatiable curiosity rather than by hunger alone. Quickly, he took two feeding crawfish before they could escape to their elaborate mud burrows among the cattails. He could not let such an easy meal go.

He patrolled the lake steadily and carefully. On the far shore, near where the cold, clear waters of Blue Cloud Spring emptied into the lake, he took two more crawfish, a small bullfrog, and perhaps a dozen of the minnows that often gathered in large schools about the sycamore's sunken roots. By midmorning he had covered that portion of the lake he considered his territory many times, and he began to work his way back to the dark safety of the wooden pier. Here, among the sunken pilings and old car tires, he rested through the long afternoon, hugging the bottom, only his gills moving. A bluegill darted out from among the tires, and the big bass gulped it down in one quick motion, without expression or effort.

Though the monsters of his tribe might grow to 3 feet in length and weigh more than 10 pounds, he was as yet only half that long and weighed but 4.5 pounds. Still, for a male largemouth bass, he was a big and handsome fish. As with other fish, among the largemouth bass, the female is larger. Indeed, usually any largemouth bass over 6 pounds is a female. In the lake's shallow reaches where the sunlight soaked his form, flashed along his heavily muscled flanks, he was a dark satiny green with darker splotches of black green running down his back and a dark band of color running from his massive jaws to his powerful tail. In the clearer water near shore, he sparkled like a rare jewel. Largemouth bass have a reputation of being aggressive and fearless opportunists. Among fish, they are bullies and malcontents, fish with a short temper that like to throw their weight around.

The heavy shadows of late afternoon edged across the old pier and out over the lake, cooling the water. He loved mornings and evenings, the water chilly, crisp, between 65 and 72 degrees Fahrenheit, the sunlight dappled and soft on the lake's surface. These last few days, though, he had felt restless, edgy, even more belligerent than usual. He stayed on the move, patrolling his territory between the pier and the sunken sycamore log as though searching for something. Though the sun was still high in the sky, again he had the urge to move. He darted quickly out from under the pier, small schools of bluegill and minnows retreating in panic as he approached. Suddenly, he was motionless, limp in the shallow water. Above him on the water's surface, a fallen cricket struggled. He rose to it quickly, without hesitation, breaking the surface, his white belly shining in the sunlight.

The cricket eaten, his mood changed. No longer the relentless hunter, his aggression was now turned to ridding his territory of every intruder from sunfish to turtle. This done, he at last found a place along the bottom to his liking and set to work in earnest. As with the other members of the sunfish family, among largemouth bass, it is the male that selects the nest site and builds the nest. He worked well toward dusk removing debris from the site with his gaping mouth and strong jaws. Using his tail as a powerful fan, he cleared an area perhaps 20 inches in diameter and about 6 inches deep. Completed, the nest looked like a small bowl of smooth, well-scrubbed gravel. The work had taken hours, and his tail was swollen and tattered. Exhausted, he retreated to the pier to rest and wait for morning.

At first light, he began to move, swimming swiftly, powerfully about the nest site he had prepared. He swam in great circles, boldly announcing his presence. With morning barely a pink smudge in the eastern sky, a heavy female crossed in front of the pier. Cautiously he approached her, his mood gentle, conciliatory.

After repeated urgings, she swam directly over the nest, let herself sink but an inch or two over its smooth floor of pebbles, and began to vent a small river of bright-orange roe, hundreds of them, each about the size of a pencil point. The sticky egg mass instantly attached itself to the stones. After several minutes she had laid perhaps a thousand of the fifty-thousand eggs she carried inside her. The rest she would lay elsewhere, over other such nest sites, or redds, prepared by other males living in the lake. With life, nature seldom takes needless risks. If laid all at one time, in one place, the female's eggs would, at best, face a bleak future. This way, surely a handful of the eggs would hatch, mature, and survive, ensuring the future of the lake's largemouth bass.

As she hovered over the nest, the male circled nervously, protecting her, driving off every intruder, no matter how small or harmless. Sure of her safety, he drifted near the nest, positioning himself slightly upstream to take advantage of the lake's small current. This done, he began fertilizing the freshly laid eggs. The female rose and swam slowly into the dark shadows of the deeper channel. The male did not follow or try to stop her. Indeed, if she should try to return, he would violently drive her off. The nest and its precious young were now under his protection. Tirelessly, he circled the nest. He would do so without food or rest until the eggs hatched.

When they emerged as small bass fry, dark little fish perhaps an inch long, the sight of them would end the male's tenure as parent. Again, he was a big and hungry bass and would devour as many of the young bass as he could catch. As for the rest, their lives would be no less precarious. Feeding on daphnia, those few that survived would go on to adulthood to roam the lake and stake out territories of their own.

The big male ate and ate, gorging himself on anything, everything he could find. He even ventured into the shallows by Blue Cloud Spring looking for bullfrogs and had to race for deep water when a large shadow swept over him. A sudden coolness, like darkness, fell over him. An owl? Perhaps, but more likely the large osprey that lived in the dead oak at the east end of the lake that he had often seen skimming the lake's surface, its great dark talons spread, poised for a strike. That he had been aware of the moving shadow in time was mostly due to his lateral scales that ran from his gills to his tail, which were extremely sensitive to vibrations and were invaluable in locating not only prey but possible enemies as well. Even in the murkiest water he could feel the tremble of water beetles on the surface above him.

Tired, he at last sought the shelter and safety of the pier. Settled on the dark bottom between sunken tires he looked up and noticed a faint ripple on the surface, then the shape of a curious looking bug, fat and black and bristly. He watched it hungrily. Then the bug jumped temptingly and again landed on the surface. The male's great tail flicked in anticipation as he rose swiftly to take the bug. He broke the surface of the water violently, gulping bug, water, air.

The hook set at once, digging into the flesh and bone of his massive jaw. In panic, he raced for the deep channel, tossing his green-and-white speckled head. He tried to escape but could not. Changing directions, he shot back up to the surface, jumped, tried desperately to be free of the hook. He thrashed and jerked, rose to the surface, jumped fearfully in the air, landing on his side and back, hoping the impact might set him free. He turned back toward the pier. He was tired now, very tired. Something was pulling him to the surface, and he was powerless to resist it. His strength was gone. He turned over on his back and lay limp in the dark water. A large hand reached down from the side of the pier, took him firmly by the gills, pulled him up, and laid him on the pier.

Late that evening, the angler took the big male with the rest of his catch, three other largemouth bass of varying sizes, and filleted them at the edge of the pier, taking the firm white meat of the flanks and casting the remains back into the lake's dark waters. The night air was soon soaked with the rich smell of frying bass, butter, garlic, and onions. Meanwhile, below the pier, a horde of bass fry had gathered to feed on the remains of the big male as the moon rose and the fisherman whistled.

(1985)

Sudden Storm

They had been building all morning, enveloping one another: rafts of clouds moored together, billowing, reaching high into the seemingly endless sprawl of West Texas sky east of Salt Flat. Brooding and ominous, charcoal gray at the edges, dark as burnt grease where the ragged peaks of the Guadalupe Mountains mark the horizon like a jagged scar, the clouds seem to hang over the land. The sky seems like a palette of smudged lampblack.

Outside Salt Flat, I pulled the truck off the highway to watch this distended sky, feel the energy of the rising storm. The wind is up, suddenly cool, heavy with the smell of rain.

The clouds spread relentlessly across the sky, a Wagnerian opera of chaotic motion expanding cathedrals of ever-changing shapes and colors, wild winds, and darkening portent.

Such storms seem as much poetry as cold, dispassionate science, as much haunting sensation as distilled facts and irrefutable certainty. Yet, facts are wrinkling beneath the swirling imagery of dark clouds. Enough to ruminate on for some time as I sit on the warm stones off the highway and watch the storm take on what feels like biblical proportions.

The evaporating moisture from lakes, rivers, oceans, even the surfaces of plants, rises. As this moisture reaches the colder upper parts of the atmosphere, ice crystals form and begin gathering about microscopic particles called condensation nuclei. These grains are so tiny that there can be more than two million particles per cubic foot of air. As the grains take on more density, they become visible clouds. For the most part the shape of clouds depends on air temperature and the amount of humidity in the surrounding atmosphere.

There are three main classifications of clouds: cirrus (curls and wisps, as fine as strands of hair), stratus (layered), and cumulus (heaps of clouds). The clouds spreading out over the Guadalupe Mountains are cumulus clouds that have mutated, while rising on the hot thermal winds coming off the mountains, into cumulonimbus clouds, clouds that herald a rage and fury of storm-tossed energy. Up high, where the great clouds flatten, their tops flat and dark as pounded anvil heads, the air currents are incredibly strong.

Gaining the top of the mountains, the cloud banks continue to rise, spiraling perhaps 30,000 to 40,000 feet into the atmosphere. Looking like stitches of gold thread on sackcloth, lightning tears great tracks across the sky.

The lightning flashes both from cloud to cloud and from the clouds to the ground. Only a small percentage of lightning actually strikes the ground, but it has no favored place; it can and will strike the same spot once or a dozen times. Lightning bolts are like great electrical pistons gone haywire. Each strike is not one but many, a tapestry of vast electrical energy called streamers, each packing perhaps 5 million volts—enough energy to light up several small towns.

Then it comes: raindrops the size of mothballs at first, splattering noisily on the truck, a drumming metallic sound, like nails being rattled in a bucket. Thunder rolls across the landscape like dinosaurian guttural groans. The wind no longer merely howls; it shoves, pushes, pummels. As the storm intensifies, the atmospheric pressure continues to drop.

For all its power and violent temper, it is but one storm of the perhaps 1,500 such thunderstorms that are pummeling the planet at any given moment on any given day. There can be as many as 40,000 such storms, some more damaging than others, a day. Imagine that: it seems we are never far from the eye of the storm.

This West Texas country is to such storms what cold, fast, clean water is to trout: the perfect breeding ground. These mountains produce ideal conditions for the development of what are called air mass thunderstorms, storms that result from hot air rising rapidly and cooling rapidly, reaching the dew point, condensing. Each storm has a topography all its own, a whirlwind geography of clouds and winds, sound and motion, and rain.

Such storms are both foreboding and awesome, frightening and beautiful, each one a dark-souled, wild symphony, something that can neither be tamed nor controlled.

As suddenly as it came, the storm finally dissipates. And there is only the wind and a cool mist coming off the highway and sunlight feathering out along the edges of mountain ridges. The land seems to shudder, and the sky glows soft purple, the color of a healing bruise.

On the truck radio the weatherman says tomorrow will be another scorcher with a good chance of afternoon thunderstorms. It will be just enough rain to settle the dust, give a moment's cool shiver to the burnt West Texas plains and man alike.

(1990)

The Bird with Brains

Natural history and quantum physics have a great many things in common. One of them is the baffling fact that there is so little hard evidence in the world to explain the world. As one physicist aptly described it: "The universe is not only queerer than we imagine, but it is queerer than we *can* imagine." And so we are faced with such astonishing and perplexing things as quarks, quantum leaps, and crows.

The problem with crows is their brains, which are larger than the brains of other birds. Man has trouble acknowledging, much less accepting, intelligence in any creature other than himself, especially if it's something as curious and plainly troubling as a crow: an oversized black bird of inextricable character, a penchant for irreverent behavior and hooliganism, and what often seems like a devilish sense of humor.

The crow's intelligence makes him sort of an avian misfit, an evolutionary oddity, more than mere bird and yet not quite anything else. Intelligence with feathers. Brains on the wing. Scientists have long felt that crows are misunderstood not only because they are such unorthodox birds but also because they are obviously too sophisticated for their station in life. Just being crows leaves them tedious, which, in turn, leads to malevolent tendencies that often lead to outlandish, even baroque, lifestyles.

Science, in an endless effort to come to grips with the crow, has observed, studied, and analyzed every aspect of its life and behavior. Crows are forever being marched into laboratories to take an ever-increasing battery of tests. The results are always astonishing and vexing. Crows have a knack for solving puzzles; they do well at keeping track of things and at tasks that involve rudimentary counting; they are fascinated by locks and will spend hours fiddling with them; they are superb mimics, especially of offbeat noises: a knock at the door, the clack of a bad engine, the creak of a rusty gate.

In short, crows do not seem pressed to act as other birds do. For them, the routine of avian life has lost some of its challenge, and they seem slightly discontent and therefore bent on expanding their interests—such as rock throwing. Crows delight in picking things up, strolling about with them, then tossing them aside, or better yet, taking flight and dropping them, as bombardiers might let loose their cargo. There's nothing sinister to this pastime. Indeed, much of it has practical applications, for crows have learned to drop such items as nuts on highways in order to make an easier meal of them. Aerial gastronomy. Crows work hard at amusing themselves, rushing excitedly from one thing to the next, whatever rouses their interminable curiosity. They have, for example, a particular weakness for the bright, the shiny, the polished—whether it's a stone, a fork, or a good -sized aluminum pie pan. Generally, they will make off with anything they can carry. Of course, it is quite unscientific and subjective to assign feelings and emotions to creatures who seem to be getting by nicely without them. But, on seeing a mature crow swinging nonchalantly by one foot from a fencepost at the edge of a meadow while yowling at no one in particular, it is hard to write the scene off as instinct rather than a simple fit of exuberance and exhilaration.

Crows are clearly trying to have a good time, set their intelligence to some use, even if it's only sitting about in suspicious groups swapping gossip and obviously plotting something mildly licentious, irresponsible, or mutinous. They are like gangs of youth, once full of potential and promise, who have somehow fallen in with the wrong company and have turned their backs on useful, productive behavior so they can hang out along roadsides and highways mimicking life, while waiting for man's automobiles to provide an easy meal. Cars, from a crow's point of view, are curious hunters—efficient, yet abandoning what they kill, leaving the roadways as packed with groceries as a supermarket.

Eccentric behavior is a family trait among crows and their kind. Crows are part of the Corvidae family, a peculiar clan of avian delinquents, which includes magpies, jays, jackdaws, and the quirky ravens. Indeed, anyone set on a greater understanding of Corvidae would be better off with a background in analytical psychology rather than in ornithology.

Despite their fits and starts, their penchant for oddball antics, crows can and do lead moderately private lives. Birds of great longevity (some live as long as twenty years or more), crows spend their days as practicing monogamists and generally mate for life. The male is something of a romantic, given to all sorts of elaborate courtship ploys, including some snappy bobbing, weaving, and dancing. To make sure his intended is getting the drift of it all, he at last shows up with a bit of nesting material in his beak. Crows are doting parents, even though mortality among the young is high. The crow believes in balance. There are never too many or too few crows, but always just enough of them.

While crows are gifted mimics, they are also talented in the vanishing art of just making noise. Crows use more than twenty different calls just to communicate or harass each other. They are more hecklers than songsters, as anyone who has spent some time listening to them will surely attest. The sound is reminiscent of a grammar school band playing military marches slightly out of key.

The common crow, certainly the least loyal of the crow family, ranges widely throughout North America, from Canada to Mexico. In size, the average adult can measure more than 20 inches in length and have a wingspan of up to 40 inches. In coloring, crows go beyond black, deeper than the somber shadings of darkness. Their feathers shine like wet coal, and in sunlight the feathers take on an iridescent glow of dark blues and bruised purples. They are more handsome than elegant; theirs is an unpretentious beauty, like twilight. No habitat is completely alien to crows, though they prefer open woodland and agricultural land because such places offer them year-round food supplies.

Crows are both gregarious and solitary. Because we tend to see them in loosely knit syndicates or groups roaming about the countryside, it is hard to think of crows as private creatures, but they can be. Only during migration do crows seek each other out in large numbers, forming huge flocks that move down from Canada and the Eastern United States to the warmer and milder wintering grounds of the South.

Crows shoulder a spoiled reputation, most of it undeserved. Even so, men have spared no expense in trying to get the best of these birds, only to be outsmarted again and again. They have hunted them and even poisoned them but to no avail. Each morning at sunrise, the crow is there letting out a loud cackle, getting in the last word.

(1989)

Coot du Jour

South of my grandfather's farm, the land gave way to a broad expanse of bottomland swamp, a dark, brooding place that no one claimed or especially wanted. Mr. Biddle, who was both a farmer and the local Methodist preacher, claimed the swamp was home to all sorts of smarmy evil, not to mention alligators and panthers and sundry other monsters.

Ellis Johns, however, liked the swamp, but then he hadn't been to church in twenty-four years and, consequently, had no idea of what waited there to do him in, soul and all. Ellis Johns enjoyed the swamp for many reasons, but chief among them was its abundance of coots. To Mr. Johns, coots were not only an interesting fowl, but they were also a source of considerable livelihood. Mr. Johns had a reputation throughout the county for his coot stew, which was hailed as much for its medicinal as its culinary distinctiveness. This was no mean achievement. Among most outdoorsmen it is an article of faith that coot simply cannot be disguised or otherwise masqueraded as something palatable. Yet Mr. Johns could turn this sorry bird into a thoroughly pleasing, even delightful soup. Sufferers from throughout the county showed up at Mr. Johns's place regularly to buy a pint jar of his famed Coot Juice. My grandfather was among Mr. Johns's customers. He once described a jigger of Coot Juice as tasting like a mix of Tabasco sauce, chicken soup, and a dash of tequila. A concoction that could open up every pore in a man's body.

The principal ingredient in Mr. Johns's elixir, of course, was coot, the American coot *(Fulica americana),* a less than admirable member, some might argue, of the rail family. Coots are hardy and populous birds. They can be found from the southern reaches of Canada south to the Baja region of Mexico. They are particularly fond of the Southern swamplands and other regions that abound in freshwater lakes and ponds and marshes.

In fashion, coots are hardly trendsetters. Perhaps their most distinguishing trait is their curious toes: they're lobed, which accounts for the coot's tremendous swimming ability. The bird is at ease as much in the water as on land. Thanks to its peculiar toes, the coot's personality isn't so much split as just well adapted.

Coots have the look of a duck but without the duck's grace. Coots can reach a foot or greater in length and sport a wingspan of between 25 and 28 inches. Their coloring is lackluster. They poke about in a frock of unpolished slate gray and are distinguished from gallinules, for whom they are often mistaken, by their short, white chunky bills.

Gallinules have flashy, handsome red bills. Coots also have a distinct white patch beneath their blunt tails. Their odd anatomy is completed by adding eyes the shade of ripe cranberries and greenish legs and feet.

Despite their comic appearance, coots are superb swimmers and divers. The grace they lack above water is displayed brilliantly below the surface. Coots feed on fronds, aquatic plants and roots, algae, small fish, tadpoles, and insects. Sociable birds, they often gather in large flocks to gossip and exchange the latest news. Open bays and bigger lakes seem to attract flocking coots more than the confines of smaller swamps and sloughs. Also, because of their size and their less than acrobatic style, coots need a rather long watery runway to get airborne.

Under the press of cold winters, coots will migrate. Consequently, during the cold months they are most abundant from Florida and the Southeast north to Maryland. Beginning in March, the birds start working their way north to mate. Courtship among coots resembles a madcap game of chase, as males display and pursue females on the water. Curiosity seems to mark coots in every department, including song. They do not produce songs; they produce sounds. Put into vocabulary, their diction goes something like this: *coo-coo . . . coo-coo,* with a few *kuk-kuk-kuk*s thrown in to spice up their repertory. Coots sound off whenever they feel like it, night or day. Once mated, coots build nests on the water, a traveling houseboat fashioned from marsh plants and grasses. Mottled-colored eggs come in April and May, and both parents incubate them. The eggs hatch in a month or less, and the chicks are on the wing after perhaps seventy-five days.

There is, naturally, nothing to fear of a swamp. Swamps are delightful, full of adventure and wonderful surprises. They should be visited and enjoyed more often. Should your travels ever take you to one and should you suddenly be assailed by a cacophony of shrieks, hoots, groans, whistles, cackles, and grunts, fear not; it's probably just an old coot: Mr. Johns's noble fowl, the cure to man's every malady.

(1990)

Southern Lights

No matter how much science discovers and deciphers about the natural world, there is always more to know, learn, and wonder about. The tangle of nature's mysteries does indeed seem endless.

There is no limit to the earth's capacity for the extraordinary. It seethes all about us—in the dazzling patterns of lightning lacing a storm-choked, late-summer night sky; in every splash of an ocean wave along the shore; in a bird's song; in a trout's rise; in a single leaf spiraling on a lazy wind to the cool, dark, damp forest floor.

In my childhood, one of the greatest moments of the earth's seasonal magic came during summer nights when the humid Arkansas sky would sparkle like a tiny galaxy with the flickering, soft, orange-yellow light of swarms of fireflies. Many a night I chased the pulsating trail of light along the edge of Barlow's Wood, through the deep, wet grass and leaves, as the glowing cloud of fireflies appeared then quickly disappeared. So many beads of light flashed in the darkness. They were, it seemed, as elusive as the wind itself.

When luck was with me, I would catch dozens of them and carefully put them in an old peanut butter jar with plenty of holes punched in its metal lid. I'd race up to my room, shut the door, set the jar on my cluttered dresser, sit on the edge of my bed, and watch in wild-eyed amazement as they would illuminate my small room with their soft, warm light. On some nights I would lie on my bed for hours staring at the jar, imagining that these distant blinking lights were not fireflies at all but the stars themselves, fading lights in a night as dark as a raven's wing. As a boy, by the way, I never called these agents of light "fireflies." To me they were lightning bugs or glowworms (actually flightless fireflies). It was only later that I learned that fireflies are not really flies or even worms. Rather, they are soft-bodied beetles of the Lampyridae family.

———◆———

Not all members of the Lampyridae family give off light. This curious gift belongs only to a relatively few species. Those that do not glow are rather innocuous common beetles that are most active in the daytime. With the sun to guide them, there is no need to produce artificial light.

Throughout most of the South, however, most species of fireflies are winged and luminescent. Both sexes glow at intervals like a slowly fed fire. This ability to glow does not end with the adults, however. Even the eggs and the larvae of the firefly are bathed in light—families of light. Entomologists pretty much agree that the firefly's light is actually little more than an illuminated Morse code that enables members of the opposite sex to locate each other at night.

Light, even the variety produced by the firefly, is not an unheard of phenomenon in the natural world. A myriad of torches glows from the mountaintops to the seashore. Much of the natural world glows. The sea brims with luminescence, from simple bacteria to some species of squid and fishes, even at the ocean's deepest depths. In the woods, the nights vibrate with every shade of the prism. Producing light is an ancient activity, but perhaps no creature has retained it, refined it, made it such an integral part of his survival and livelihood as the firefly. The adults have the most advanced light-producing organs known in the natural world, and even today they remain complex, not completely known or understood. Even man has trouble matching the firefly's lighting efficiency; for despite their size, fireflies produce a great deal of light while giving off little heat. Theirs is a cold light. While they set the summer skies on fire, they expend virtually no energy. Now there is true sleight of hand.

Ulisse Aldrovandi, one of the first scientists to pay much attention to the firefly, believed that the insect used its light like a signal fire to find its way through the night. Aldrovandi set forth this theory in his *De Animalibus Insectis* (1602), which many scientists mark as the beginning of serious insect observation and study. Aldrovandi's speculation about the firefly held sway until another Italian scientist, Vintimillia, proved that the firefly's flickering light was indeed a beaming aphrodisiac.

Then in the nineteenth century, Raphael Dubois, a French physiologist, discovered from his work with the luminescent beetle Pyrophorus that two substances were needed for the beetle to produce light. These Dubois called luciferin and luciferase, both named after Lucifer, the bearer not only of evil but of light as well.

Today, science has learned to synthesize both these substances. It has also been learned that Dubois missed one essential ingredient in the firefly's ability to produce light—ATP or adenosine triphosphate, a chemical necessary, even in human beings, for muscle contraction. In the firefly, it is the ATP that provides the energy for the beetle's lighting system.

As for the firefly's magnificent cold light, scientists believe it begins first as a nervous impulse from the firefly's tiny brain, actually no more than a bundle of nerves. This impulse then travels the length of the insect's central nervous system to luminous cells located behind the abdomen. How and why the firefly's light flashes is still not exactly known. This much, however, is known. The beetle's light organ has three layers—an outer layer, which is transparent; an interior layer of opaque reflector cells; and a layer of larger cells where the ATP is stored.

The nature of these light organs and even the color of the light produced varies from species to species. A firefly's light can range in color from a pinpoint of brilliant white light to a soft, diffused light of yellow, and even pale blue. Different levels of luciferase seem directly responsible for this wonderful range of light, this display of firefly fireworks.

How a firefly will react to light depends on what species it is. In most of the South, for example, female fireflies rest on the ground or on some piece of grass and respond to the male's coded light messages. Of course, there are exceptions. Some female fireflies have learned to mimic the blinking codes of other species and are able to entice unsuspecting males to them. But normally the female firefly will sit waiting patiently for the male's signal. The male, flying in a spiraling I-pattern flashes his light every four to six seconds. If he is close to a female of his species, she will respond, announcing her position like a brief flare shining in the night. Clearly, a firefly is known by the flash, the color, and the duration of its light. The light is a badge, a calling card, proof of identification, like fingerprints.

But none of this scientific information strips the firefly of its magic and its wonder. Often on muggy summer nights down by the river, I still watch clusters of darting fireflies dancing among the oaks and hickories and bursting into light like a series of strobes. It is a marvelous light, one that glows like a waning moon and briefly lights up the riverbank. The big barred owls hoot, the wind moves through the trees, and I sit nearby watching, full of wonder as if I have stumbled onto some wild, magical, private fireworks display. Even though I know the source of their light, the magic is not broken. On such nights, I feel as though I am lying on my back and the sky is alive with shooting stars.

(1987)

Bibliography

In That Sweet Country is a collection of Harry Middleton's writings that appeared previously in the following publications: *Blair & Ketchum's Country Journal, Field & Stream, The Flyfisher, Fly Fishing News, Fly Rod & Reel, Gray's Sporting Journal,* the *New York Times, Sierra, Southern Living, Southpoint,* and *Sports Illustrated.*

ARKANSAS
The Fisherman
From *Blair & Ketchum's Country Journal* (April 1983)
First Fish
From *Southern Living* (April 1990)
Downriver, Again
From *Blair & Ketchum's Country Journal* (May 1981)

Classic Cane

From *Fly Rod & Reel* (January/February 1989)

WINGS, WIND & WONDER

The Song of the Whippoorwill

From *Southern Living* (February 1989)

The Rising Bass

From *Southern Living* (April 1985)

Sudden Storm

From *Southern Living* (September 1990)

The Bird with Brains

From *Southern Living* (October 1989)

Coot du Jour

From *Southern Living* (March 1990)

Southern Lights

From *Southern Living* (August 1987)

About the Authors

HARRY MIDDLETON (1949–1993) lived in Birmingham, Alabama, with his wife, Marcy, and two sons, Travis and Sean, at the time of his untimely death, on July 28, 1993. As a senior editor and nature editor for *Southern Living* magazine, he wrote the monthly "Outdoors South" column and numerous features, from 1984 to 1991, while contributing stories, essays, and book reviews to numerous periodicals, including *Sports Illustrated*, the *New York Times, Gray's Sporting Journal, Field & Stream, Fly Rod & Reel*, and *Sierra*, among others. Harry Middleton left an impressive body of work rich in mountains, wild trout, cold mountain water, and the wonderful characters he discovered while frequenting the country he most loved. He is best remembered for his books *The Earth is Enough* (1989), *On the Spine of Time* (1991), and *The Bright Country* (1993), all of which are still published in paperback by Pruett Publishing Company in Boulder, Colorado. Two first-edition hardback volumes, Pruett Publishing's *Rivers of Memory* (1993) and Meadow Run Press's limited-edition *The Starlight Creek Angling Society* (1992), are out-of-print and highly sought after by collectors.

Ron Ellis is the author of *Cogan's Woods* and *Brushes with Nature: The Art of Ron Van Gilder* and the editor of *Of Woods and Waters: A Kentucky Outdoors Reader*. His stories have appeared in *The Gigantic Book of Hunting Stories*, *Sporting Classics*, *Kentucky Afield*, *Kentucky Monthly*, and in *Afield: American Writers on Bird Dogs*. He lives in Kentucky with his wife and son.